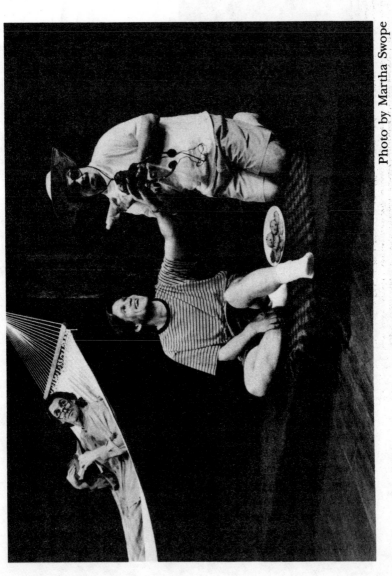

Photo by Martha Swope

John Glover, Anthony Heald and Nathan Lane in a scene from the Broadway production of "Love! Valour! Compassion!". Set design by Loy Arcenas.

LOVE!
VALOUR!
COMPASSION!

BY TERRENCE McNALLY

★

★

DRAMATISTS
PLAY SERVICE
INC.

For Nathan Lane

Great heart
Great soul
Great actor
Best friend

AUTHOR'S NOTE

Plays are meant to be seen, not read, and yet we playwrights are always moaning how difficult it is to get our plays published. In fact, we moan about that almost as much as we moan how difficult it is to get our plays produced. Of course, the thing we moan about most is how difficult it is to write them.

That's a lot of moaning.

The truth is probably that none of it has ever been easy — writing, production or publication — but in these last fleeting moments of the twentieth century the voices of those who claim that the theater is not only dying but actually dead and just doesn't know it yet are particularly strident and, to some ears, persuasive, so that a single playwright's moans may seem just that more poignant and urgent than in Shakespeare's day or in Ibsen's.

Significantly, none of those voices belongs to a working playwright. Our moans are pretty small potatoes by comparison. They're saying the party's over; we're saying give us the opportunity and we'll show you it's just begun. A lot of very good plays are being written right now. They're being produced; they're even being published. The only thing they're not is easier to write.

Very few of them are being produced on Broadway, however, which has led to the false conclusion that they aren't being written at all. Not true. The American theater has never been healthier. It's Broadway that's sick. The American theater is no longer Broadway. It is Los Angeles, it is Seattle, it is Louisville, it is everywhere but the west side of midtown Manhattan.

Just look around. For the first time in our history, we have a *national* theater — regional theaters are in the vanguard of producing the world premieres of our best playwrights. Twenty-five years ago regional theaters produced New York's hits, period. Now New York is host to the best work of the not-for-profit regional theater.

I was recently asked to appear on a panel saluting "The Golden Age of Gay Theatre." Nonsense. This is a golden age for the American theater, gay *and* straight. The good new plays are being written and produced as I write this introduction. Take it from someone who toils in the trenches: The energy being generated by American playwrights, directors, actors and designers is seismic. With a little luck you'll be reading about them and seeing them and reading them by this time next year. With no luck at all you'll be aware of them in two or three or maybe five years, but I promise you, they're coming soon to a theater near you. The American theater is on a roll, and there is no stopping us.

I wouldn't be a playwright today if it weren't for the regional theater. My regional theater is the Manhattan Theatre Club. I'm a regional theater playwright who just happens to live in New York.

Without the unconditional love of MTC (*support* seems too meager a word), this play would never have been written. Knowing that they are committed to me as a writer and not as a playwright who is expected to provide them with "hits" has given me the confidence to write each play as I wanted, not what I think *they* wanted based on expectations from the last play. Thanks to MTC I don't have to compete with myself. There was never any danger that I would be tempted to write *Lips Together, Teeth Apart 2* or *Frankie and Johnny Go to Paris* or *Revenge of the Lisbon Traviata.*

And while I write and dream my next play, I know that I will have a production of it at MTC regardless of its likelihood to succeed with audiences and critics. I may be the only playwright in America who has such an arrangement with a producing theater. Because of it, I know I am the luckiest. I owe Lynne Meadow, Barry Grove and Michael Bush my artistic life. In a profession strewn with too many orphans, they have given me a home that in truth feels more like a fairy tale palace. I have a theater!

Good fortune has allowed me to work with the best actors, directors and designers of these times. The play in hand is no exception. *Love! Valour! Compassion!* had no specific moment of inspiration. The title comes from an entry in John Cheever's journals. I think I wanted to write about what it's like to be a gay man at this particular moment in our history. I think I wanted to tell my friends how much they've meant to me. I think I wanted to tell everyone else who we are when they aren't around. I think I wanted to reach out and let more people into those places in my heart where I don't ordinarily welcome strangers. I think a lot of things about this play, but mainly I think it's much too soon to know what they are. These things take time.

I know for certain, however, that the play was given a definitive production by Joe Mantello and seven remarkable actors: Nathan Lane, Stephen Spinella, John Glover, Stephen Bogardus, John Benjamin Hickey, Justin Kirk and Randy Becker. Loy Arcenas took an impossible design situation and made it seem as easy as it was inevitable.

Manhattan Theatre Club had done it again for me. No wonder I have never been tempted, not once, in all these years, to roam. I like to think I'm smart, too.

So once again I am wallowing in some kind of playwright's heaven. If I'm not careful, I'll forget to moan. This book should have come out months ago. The *Love! Valour! Compassion!* cast hasn't been signed to life-indenturing contracts. The theater was too cold last night. The night before, it was too hot. There, that feels much better. The truth is, I'm worrying about the next play. Will it be any good? What's really scary is that Manhattan Theatre Club will produce it all the same. I have no one to blame if it fails but me. That's terrifying.

Moaning is easier.

— TERRENCE McNALLY
New York City, 1995

LOVE! VALOUR! COMPASSION! was originally produced at the Manhattan Theatre Club (Lynne Meadows, Artistic Director; Barry Groves, Managing Director), in New York City, on November 1, 1994. It was directed by Joe Mantello; the set design was by Loy Arcenas; the costume design was by Jess Goldstein; the lighting design was by Brian MacDevitt; the sound design was by John Kilgore; the choreography was by John Carrafa; the production stage manager was William Joseph Barnes and the stage manager was Ira Mont. The cast was as follows:

GREGORY MITCHELL	Stephen Bogardus
ARTHUR PAPE	John Benjamin Hickey
PERRY SELLARS	Stephen Spinella
JOHN JECKYLL/JAMES JECKYLL	John Glover
BUZZ HAUSER	Nathan Lane
BOBBY BRAHMS	Justin Kirk
RAMON FORNOS	Randy Becker

The production subsequently transferred to Broadway as a Manhattan Theatre Club presentation, by special arrangement with Jujamcyn Theaters. It opened at the Walter Kerr Theatre on January 20, 1995. The only cast replacement was Anthony Heald in the role of Perry Sellars.

THE PLAYERS

BOBBY BRAHMS, early twenties
RAMON FORNOS, early twenties
BUZZ HAUSER, mid-thirties
JOHN JECKYLL, late forties
JAMES JECKYLL, his twin
GREGORY MITCHELL, early forties
ARTHUR PAPE, late thirties, early forties
PERRY SELLARS, late thirties, early forties

THE SETTING

A remote house and wooded grounds by a lake in Dutchess County, two hours north of New York City.

THE TIME

The present. Memorial Day, Fourth of July, and Labor Day weekends, respectively.

LOVE! VALOUR!
COMPASSION!

ACT ONE

Bare stage.

There are invisible doors and traps in the walls and floor.

Lights up.

The seven actors are singing "Beautiful Dreamer" by Stephen Foster to a piano accompaniment.

Gregory turns out and addresses us.

GREGORY. Um. I love my. Um. House. Everybody does. I like to fill it with my friends. Um. And walk around the grounds at night and watch them. Um. Through the lighted windows. It makes me happy to see them inside. Um. Our home. Mine. Um. And Bobby's. Um. I'm sorry. Um. I don't do this. Um. On purpose. Um.

ARTHUR. It's okay, Gregory.

GREGORY. It was built in 1915 and still has most of the. Um. Original roof. The wallpaper in the dining room. Um. Is original, too. So is. Um. A lot of the cabinet work. You'd have to be a fool. Um. To change it. This sofa is my pride. Um. And joy. It came with the house. It's genuine. Um. Horsehair. It's itchy but I don't care. I love it.

PERRY. Tell them about the sled.

GREGORY. Jerome Robbins gave me this sled.

PERRY. Mutual admiration, he said. One master choreographer to another.

GREGORY. It's flat here, I said. No hills. Um. What am I going to do with a sled? It's not a sled, Gregory, he told me. It's an antique.

JOHN. It's not an antique, Gregory. It's a piece of junk.

GREGORY. I hope you. Um. Appreciate detail. That. Um. Wainscoting there. This finial here. The main stairs. Um. Have a very gentle rise. Everyone comments how easy it is to. Um. Climb them.

BUZZ. I love your stairs, Gregory. They're so easy.

ARTHUR. Don't tease him like that.

BUZZ. Who's teasing? I wasn't teasing!

GREGORY. They don't build houses like this anymore. Um. The golden age. Um. Of American house building.

BUZZ. If this is going to be Pick On Buzz weekend...!

GREGORY. Not architecture, mind you, but house building. This house. Um. Was meant. Um. To stand. Welcome. Make yourself at home. *(As the men begin to break apart and drift to their various bedrooms, we see that two of them are kissing furiously: Bobby and Ramon.)*

BOBBY. No. No. No. *(They continue. Now it is Perry who turns to us.)*

PERRY. Anyway. Bobby had gone downstairs for cookies, Pepperidge Farm Brussels, and a glass of milk. Whether Ramon had followed him or was waiting for him, quiet like a cat, bare feet cold on the bare wood floors, I don't know. I was upstairs, asleep with my Arthur.

BUZZ. I was upstairs, asleep with myself. All this I heard later that summer — when everything changed, for good and bad but forever — but I wouldn't have been surprised.

BOBBY. Don't. Stop. Please. *(They continue.)*

PERRY. Anyway. I prefer the latter: the waiting. It implies certainty. That Bobby would wake up and steal from Gregory's bed and make his way down to their country kitchen —

BUZZ. Which actually was in the country. You're in Dutchess County, two hours north of the city.

PERRY. — and feel unfamiliar arms surround his bare chest from behind, raking his nipples, and in his surprise drop the

milk bottle and break it — *(Sound of a bottle of milk breaking.)*
GREGORY. Bobby?
PERRY. — splattering milk and shards of glass everywhere
— *(A pool of spilt milk is forming around them.)*
ARTHUR. What was that?
PERRY. — pinning them to that spot where they found
themselves in the dull light of the still-open Frigidaire door.
(John sits up in bed.)
JOHN. Ramon?
BOBBY. Just tell me, who is this? *(Ramon whispers in his ear.)*
PERRY. What name did Ramon whisper in Bobby's ear that
first night? His? One of the others'? Mine? *(One by one the other
four men resume singing.)* Anyway. They stood like this for quite
some time and achieved some sort of satisfaction. After he'd
come, Ramon whispered more words of love and passion into
Bobby's ear, and stole quietly back up the stairs and into the
bed he was sharing with John.
JOHN. Where were you?
RAMON. I couldn't sleep.
PERRY. Bobby cleaned up the mess on the kitchen floor,
the whole time wondering what an episode like this meant,
if, indeed, it meant anything at all. *(Arthur has come into the
kitchen area.)*
ARTHUR. What happened?
BOBBY. Perry?
PERRY. That's me.
ARTHUR. It's Arthur.
PERRY. Arthur's my lover. We're often —
ARTHUR. What happened?
PERRY. It's very annoying.
BOBBY. Be careful. There might be broken glass.
ARTHUR. I'm okay, I'm wearing slippers.
PERRY. Arthur is always wearing slippers.
BOBBY. I think I got it all. Did I?
ARTHUR. I can't tell.
PERRY. Bobby is blind.
ARTHUR. Do you mind if I turn the light on? I'm sorry.
BOBBY. It's all right.

PERRY.   People are always saying things like that to him. Me, too, and I've known him since he and Gregory got together. Bobby doesn't seem to mind. He has a remarkably loving nature.

ARTHUR.   You know the refrigerator door is open?

BOBBY.   Thanks. I was just going up. That's all we needed: a refrigerator filled with spoiled food and a house full of guests.

PERRY.   See what I mean? Never puts himself first. I don't understand people like that.

ARTHUR.   You're not going anywhere. Sit.

BOBBY.   What's the matter?

ARTHUR.   You cut yourself. Hang on, I'll be right back.

BOBBY.   I'm fine.

ARTHUR.   Sit. *(Arthur turns his back to Bobby. We hear running water and the sound of a piece of cloth being torn to make a bandage.)* I read an article that said most blind people hated to be helped.

BOBBY.   We love to be helped. We hate to be patronized. It's people assuming we want help that pisses us off. I'm standing at a corner waiting for the light to change and some jerk grabs my elbow and says, "Don't worry, I've got you." It happens all the time. People think blindness is the most awful thing that can happen to a person. Hey, I've got news for everybody: it's not.

PERRY.   I'm not in this conversation. I'm upstairs sleeping in the spoon position with my Arthur. Well, thinking I'm sleeping in the spoon position with my Arthur. Arthur's down in the kitchen expressing his remarkably loving nature to Bobby. *(Perry goes to his and Arthur's bed. He hugs a pillow and tries to sleep.)*

BOBBY.   "Really, I'm fine," I said.

PERRY.   I would have taken him at his word. When someone tells me he's fine, I believe him. But now we're getting Arthur's Mother Teresa.

GREGORY.   Don't make yourself sound so cynical, Perry.

PERRY.   That's Gregory expressing his remarkably loving nature. Shut up and go back to sleep. It was nothing. *(Gregory*

14

rolls over.)

JOHN.   Americans confuse sentimentality with love.

PERRY.   That's John, expressing his fundamentally hateful one. *(John is standing with his back to us. We hear the sound of him relieving himself as he turns over his shoulder and addresses Perry, who is trying to sleep.)*

JOHN.   It's true, duck. *(Arthur turns around.)*

ARTHUR.   I'll try not to hurt. *(He kneels and begins to dress Bobby's foot. Arthur is attracted to Bobby.)*

BOBBY.   Ow!

ARTHUR.   Sorry.

PERRY.   John is sour. He wrote a musical once. No one liked it. There or here. I don't know why they brought it over.

JOHN.   Retaliation for losing the War of Independence. *(He follows Ramon.)*

PERRY.   He's usually funnier than that.

JOHN.   I missed you. I said I missed you.

RAMON.   I heard you. Ssshh. Go back to sleep.

JOHN.   *Te quiero, Ramon Fornos. Te quiero.*

PERRY.   Does everyone know what that means? "I love you, Ramon Fornos. I love you." Anyway, the show closed, John stayed.

JOHN.   Some people liked it. Some people rather liked it a lot, in fact. Not many, but some. The good people.

RAMON.   Hey, c'mon, it's late!

PERRY.   He's Gregory's rehearsal pianist now. When he's not pounding out *The Rite of Spring* for Gregory's dancers, he's working on a new musical-theater project for himself.

JOHN.   The life of Houdini. It's got endless possibilities. I've written thirteen songs.

PERRY.   John is always working on a new musical-theater project, I should hasten to add.

JOHN.   What do you mean, you "should hasten to add"? Is that a crack?

RAMON.   I'm going to find another bed if you keep this up.

PERRY.   Anyway!

BUZZ.   *(Stirring.)* Did somebody say something about musicals? I distinctly heard something about musicals. Somebody

15

somewhere is talking about musicals! *(He sits up with a start. Perry holds him.)* I was having a musical comedy nightmare. They were going to revive *The King and I* for Tommy Tune and Elaine Stritch. We've got to stop them!

PERRY.   Buzz liked John's musical.

BUZZ.   It had a lot of good things in it.

PERRY.   Buzz likes musicals, period.

BUZZ.   I'm just a Gershwin with a Romberg rising in the house of Kern.

PERRY.   *(To us.)* He's off.

BUZZ.   I was conceived after a performance of *Wildcat* with Lucille Ball. I don't just love Lucy, I owe my very existence to her. For those of you who care but don't know, *Wildcat* was a musical by Cy Coleman and Carolyn Leigh with a book by N. Richard Nash. It opened December 16, 1960, at the Alvin Theatre and played for 172 performances. Two of its most-remembered songs are "Hey, Look Me Over!" and "Give a Little Whistle." For those of you who care but know all that, I'm sorry. For those of you who don't know and don't care, I'm really sorry. You're going to have a lot of trouble with me. So what's up, doc?

PERRY.   Buzz, you weren't awake for this.

BUZZ.   If I was, I don't remember it.

PERRY.   You weren't.

BUZZ.   Okay. *(He rolls over and goes back to sleep.)*

PERRY.   If it isn't about musicals, Buzz has the attention span of a very small moth. That wasn't fair. Buzz isn't well. He makes costumes for Gregory's company and does volunteer work at an AIDS clinic in Chelsea. He says he's going to find the cure for this disease all by himself and save the world for love and laughter.

BUZZ.   It sounds ridiculous when you say it like that!

PERRY.   I know. I'm sorry. *(He kisses Buzz on the head, goes back to his own bed, picks up a pillow, and hugs it close to him.)* None of us were awake for this. *(Gentle snoring begins — or humming, maybe. Arthur has stopped bandaging Bobby's foot. He is just looking at him now. His hand goes out and would touch Bobby's bare chest or arms or legs, but doesn't.)*

BOBBY.   What are you doing?

ARTHUR.   I guess you should know: there's a rather obvious stain on your pajamas.

BOBBY.   Thanks.

ARTHUR.   I didn't know I could still blush at my age.

BOBBY.   That's okay. Your secret is safe with me.

ARTHUR.   So is yours.

BOBBY.   I'm the one who should be blushing, only blind men don't blush.

ARTHUR.   That sounds like the title of one of Perry's detective novels.

BOBBY.   I had sort of an accident.

ARTHUR.   What you had was a mortal sin. I hope you both did. You know what we used to call them back in Catholic boys' school? Nocturnal emissions. It's so much nicer than "wet dream." It always made me think of Chopin. Nocturnal Emission in C-sharp Minor.

BOBBY.   I don't want Greg to know.

ARTHUR.   I swear to God, I only came down here for a glass of milk.

BOBBY.   I swear to God, I did, too.

ARTHUR.   We don't have to have this conversation at three a.m. We don't have to have this conversation ever.

BOBBY.   Okay.

ARTHUR.   We can talk about you and Greg. We can talk about me and Perry. We can talk about John and his new friend. We could even go back to bed.

BOBBY.   It was Ramon.

ARTHUR.   I figured.

BOBBY.   Why?

ARTHUR.   Who else would it be?

BOBBY.   I shouldn't have. I'm not very strong that way.

ARTHUR.   Most people aren't. *(They start walking up the stairs to their bedrooms.)*

BOBBY.   Is he attractive?

ARTHUR.   I'm not supposed to notice things like that. I'm in a relationship.

BOBBY.   So am I. Is he?

17

ARTHUR.   I think the word is "hot," Bobby. Okay? I love these stairs. They're so easy.

BOBBY.   Everyone says that. Have you ever...? On Perry...?

ARTHUR.   Yes. I don't recommend it.

BOBBY.   Did he find out?

ARTHUR.   No, I told him and it's never been the same. It's terrific, but it's not the same. Here we are. End of the line. *(He looks at Bobby.)* Don't fuck up. You are so.... *(He hugs Bobby.)* He's not that hot, Bobby. No one is.

BOBBY.   I know. Thanks. Goodnight. *(He goes into Gregory's room. Gregory is awake. Arthur joins Perry in their room. Perry is still clutching his pillow.)*

GREGORY.   Are you all right?

BOBBY.   Ssshh. Go to sleep.

ARTHUR.   Sorry. *(He lies next to Perry.)*

GREGORY.   Where were you?

ARTHUR.   Bobby cut himself.

BOBBY.   Downstairs.

ARTHUR.   He dropped a milk bottle.

BOBBY.   I cut myself.

ARTHUR.   Remember milk bottles?

BOBBY.   I dropped a milk bottle. *(He lies next to Gregory.)*

ARTHUR.   Only Gregory would have milk bottles.

GREGORY.   Are you — ?

BOBBY.   I'm fine. Arthur took care of me. Go to sleep.

ARTHUR.   Are you awake?

GREGORY.   I missed you. *(Bobby snuggles against Gregory.)*

BOBBY.   Ssshh. *(Arthur rolls over, his back to Perry now. Buzz and Ramon are snoring.)*

ARTHUR.   He is so young, Perry!

GREGORY.   I had a dream. We were in Aspen. The company. We were doing *Wesendonck Lieder.*

ARTHUR.   I wanted to hold him.

GREGORY.   The record got stuck during "Der Engel." *(Music starts.)* I had to do it over and over and over.

ARTHUR.   Desire is a terrible thing. I'm sorry we're not young anymore. *(Gregory begins to sing: very softly, not well, and never fully awake.)*

GREGORY.   In der Kindheit frühen Tagen
          Hört'ich oft von Engeln sagen,
(John sits up, while Ramon sleeps beside him, and listens. Gregory is beginning to drift off. At the same time we will hear a soprano singing the same words, her voice gently accompanying his.)
          die des Himmels hehre Wonne,
          tauschen mit der Erdensonne...
(Gregory sleeps. He and Bobby roll over in each other's arms. John has left Ramon and come out of their room. The soprano continues. All the men are snoring now.)
JOHN.   I am that merry wanderer of the night. Curiosity, a strange house, an unfaithful bedfellow drive me. Oh, there are other distractions, too, of course. A dog barking in the distance. Bed springs creaking; perhaps love is being made on the premises. The drip of the toilet on the third floor. Can they not hear it? But it's mainly the curiosity. I am obsessed with who people really are. They don't tell us, so I must know their secrets. *(Buzz moans in his sleep.)* I see things I shouldn't: Buzz is sleeping in a pool of sweat. They've increased his medication again. And for what? He's dead. *(He puts his hand on Buzz's shoulder, then moves to where Perry and Arthur are sleeping.)* Arthur has begun to sleep with his back to Perry, who clutches a pillow instead. I overhear what was better left unsaid: Arthur's sad confession of inappropriate desire. I read words I often wish were never written. Words that other eyes were never meant to see. *(He moves to where Gregory and Bobby are sleeping, takes up a journal, and reads.)* "Memorial Day Weekend. Manderley. Out here alone to work on the new piece. We've invited a full house and they're predicting rain. We'll see if Fred Avens has fixed that leak on the north side porch this time. Thought he would never get around to taking down the storm windows and putting up the screens. The garden is late. Only the cukes will be ready. Everything else will have to come from the A&P." This isn't quite what I had in mind. *(Buzz appears. He is carrying a knapsack.)*
BUZZ.   Where is everybody?
JOHN.   Did you know Gregory has only three places he feels safe? His work, in Bobby's arms, and in his journal.

BUZZ. That's disgusting.

JOHN. What is? The weather? Or the startling unoriginality of naming your house Manderley, after a kitsch-classic movie?

BUZZ. Reading someone's journal.

JOHN. Did you just get here?

BUZZ. Yes. Where's Gregory?

JOHN. Down by the lake. Are you alone?

BUZZ. No, I have Michael J. Fox in here. Are you?

JOHN. No. "I've rounded up. Um. The usual suspects. Um."

BUZZ. That's not funny. You're a guest in his home.

JOHN. "I think I'll make my special ginger soy vegetable loaf Sunday night." You see why I do this? Gregory's cooking. There's still time to buy steaks.

BUZZ. If I thought you'd ever read anything I wrote when we were together, I'd kill you. I mean it.

JOHN. "I'm stuck on the new piece. Maybe the Webern was a bad choice of music."

BUZZ. I hate what you're doing. *(He grabs the journal from John.)*

JOHN. I'm puzzled. What kind of statement about his work do you think a choreographer is making by living with a blind person?

BUZZ. I don't know and I don't care. It's not a statement. It's a relationship. Remember them?

JOHN. Nevertheless, the one can't see what the other does. Gregory's work is the deepest expression of who he is — or so one would hope — and Bobby's never seen it.

BUZZ. That's their business. At least they've got someone.

JOHN. Speak for yourself.

BUZZ. So you got lucky this weekend. Don't rub it in. Who is he? Anyone I know?

JOHN. I doubt it.

BUZZ. Is he cute?

JOHN. Yes.

BUZZ. I hate you. I really hate you. What does he do?

JOHN. He's a dancer.

BUZZ. How long have you been seeing him?

JOHN. Three weeks.

BUZZ.   Is it serious?

JOHN.   In three weeks?

BUZZ.   I get serious in about three seconds. People say "What's your rush?" I say, "What's your delay?"

JOHN.   What happened to you and — ?

BUZZ.   I got too intense for him. That's my problem with people. I'm too intense for them. I need someone like Dennis Hopper. A cute, young, gay Dennis Hopper. In the meantime, I'm through with love and all it meant to me.

JOHN.   Are you going to be holding that when they come back? *(Buzz hasn't resisted stealing a glance at Gregory's journal.)*

BUZZ.   Perry's work for Greg is *pro bono*?

JOHN.   Arts advocacy is very in.

BUZZ.   He does the clinic, too.

JOHN.   So is AIDS. I'm sorry.

BUZZ.   That's five dollars. Anyone who mentions AIDS this summer, it'll cost them.

JOHN.   Who made this rule up?

BUZZ.   I did. It's for the kitty. Cough it up. *(John holds his hand out for the journal.)*

BUZZ.   Did you?

JOHN.   Did I what?

BUZZ.   Ever read anything I wrote?

JOHN.   I don't know. Probably. I don't remember. If you left it out, yes.

BUZZ.   I would hardly call a journal left on someone's desk in their own room in their own home while they took the other guests swimming "out." *(He returns the journal.)*

JOHN.   People who keep journals — thank you — expect them to be read by people like me. They just pretend they don't. Freud was on to them like that! *(He snaps his fingers while continuing to skim the pages of the journal. We hear thunder. It will increase.)*

BUZZ.   Shit, it's going to rain.

JOHN.   Here's something about you.

BUZZ.   I don't want to hear it.

JOHN.   "It's Buzz's birthday. We got him an out-of-print recording of an obscure musical called *Seventeen.*"

21

BUZZ. I have *Seventeen.*

JOHN. "They assured us he wouldn't have it."

BUZZ. Don't worry, I'll act surprised.

JOHN. "It cost seventy-five dollars." You better act more than surprised.

BUZZ. I just paid a hundred and a quarter for it. They said it was the last copy.

JOHN. Calm down. You can exchange it.

BUZZ. For what? *CALL ME MADAM?* I mean, how many copies of a forgotten musical that opened in 1951 and ran 182 performances at the Broadhurst Theatre are they going to sell in one week? Do you know what the odds are against this sort of thing? This is like the time Tim Sheahan and Claude Meade both got me *Whoop-Up!* (*John has resumed reading in the journal, but Buzz continues, speaking to us.*) You may wonder why I fill my head with such trivial-seeming information. First of all, it isn't trivial to me, and second, I can contain the world of the Broadway musical. Get my hands around it, so to speak. Be the master of one little universe. Besides, when I'm alone, it gives me great pleasure to sing and dance around the apartment. I especially like "Big Spender" from *Sweet Charity* and "I'm Going Back Where I Can Be Me" from *Bells Are Ringing.* I could never do this with anyone watching, of course. Even a boyfriend, if I had one, which I don't. I'd be too inhibited.

So, when I'm not at the clinic thinking I am single-handedly going to find the cure for this fucking scourge (it doesn't sound ridiculous when I say it, not to me!), I am to be found at my place in Chelsea doing "Rose's Turn" from *GYPSY.* I can't think of the last time I didn't cry myself to sleep. Hey, it's no skin off your nose.

I think that is so loathsome of you, John.

(*Gregory and Ramon return from swimming.*)

GREGORY. Hello! We're back! Where is. Um. Everybody?

JOHN. I'd better return this.

BUZZ. We're up here.

GREGORY. John?

JOHN. Coming.

GREGORY. You don't know. Um. What you're missing. The lake is. Um. Wonderful.

RAMON. Don't believe him. It's freezing! *(He drops his towel.)* *¡Ay! ¡Coño! ¡Madre de Dios!*

GREGORY. Did. Um. The others get here?

JOHN. Just Buzz!

BUZZ. Hello.

GREGORY. Buzz!

RAMON. My nuts. Where are they? I have no nuts. They're gone.

GREGORY. They're not gone. Um. They're just. Um. Hiding. *(John and Buzz have returned.)*

RAMON. I had enormous nuts. I was famous for my nuts. Where are my fabulous nuts?

JOHN. I warned you, sweetheart. They got so cold in Gregory's lake they fell off and one of those goddamn snapping turtles is eating them as we speak.

GREGORY. My turtles don't. Um. Snap, Ramon. This is Buzz.

RAMON. Hi, Buzz. I had balls. He doesn't believe me. Tell him about my balls, John.

JOHN. Ramon had legendary balls up until twenty minutes ago.

BUZZ. I know. I've been following them for the last two seasons. From a tiny performance space in the East Village all the way to the Opera House at BAM. The three of you have come a long way, baby.

JOHN. Do you believe this man and I were an item?

BUZZ. A wee item, Ramon.

JOHN. You don't want to go there, Buzz.

BUZZ. But seriously (and don't you hate people who begin sentences "But seriously"?), are you guys going to be back at the Joyce? That last piece was sensational.

GREGORY. You mean *Verklärte Nacht?*

BUZZ. Speak English! The man can barely get a whole sentence out and then he hits us with *Verklärte Nacht!* *(Then to Ramon:)* I don't suppose you want to get married?

RAMON. No, but thank you.

23

BUZZ. Just thought I'd get it out there. Anyway, *Verklärte Schmatta,* whatever it is, was a thrilling piece. It blew me away. And you were fantastic.

RAMON. Thank you.

BUZZ. Your balls weren't bad, either. I stood.

GREGORY. It was wonderful work. Wonderful. Um. Energy.

RAMON. You saw us, Mr. Mitchell?

GREGORY. I wanted to know. Um. What all the. Um. Shouting was about.

RAMON. I would have freaked if I'd known you were out there, Mr. Mitchell.

GREGORY. It's Gregory, please. You're making me feel. Um. Like. Um. An old man with "Mr. Mitchell." It was great. You reminded me. Um. Of me. Um. At your age.

BUZZ. "So what's next for you guys?" he asked in a casual, bantering voice, though his heart was beating so hard he was sure everyone could hear it.

RAMON. Right now we're all just hoping there will be a next season. We're broke.

GREGORY. Every company is, Ramon.

RAMON. Not yours, surely.

BUZZ. It's "Gregory." He doesn't like "Shirley." I'm sorry. Ignore me.

JOHN. He is.

BUZZ. What you people need is a Diaghilev.

RAMON. What's a Diaghilev?

BUZZ. A rich older man who in return for certain favors funds an entire ballet company.

RAMON. Where is this rich older dude? I'm all his.

JOHN. Don't you want to know what these favors are first?

RAMON. I'm a big boy. I have a pretty good idea.

GREGORY. I'm in line first for him, Ramon.

BUZZ. Gregory, your dancers love you. We all do. We'd work for you for free.

GREGORY. I won't let you. Artists should be paid.

RAMON. Right on. The only thing an artist should do for free is make love.

JOHN. Now you tell me. Now he tells me! This is getting

entirely too artsy-fartsy/idealistic/intellectual for me. Can we go upstairs and fuck?

GREGORY. I'm going to start. Um. Dinner. They should be here soon. I thought. Um. I'd make my special. Um. *Penne Primavera. (He goes.)*

BUZZ. I brought those sketches you wanted. I've got everyone in Lycra. Lots and lots of Lycra. I'm entering my Lycra period. You still know how to clear a room, John. *(He goes.)*

RAMON. I didn't appreciate that fucking remark in front of your friends.

JOHN. I don't appreciate you flapping your dick in everybody's face, okay? Are you coming upstairs?

RAMON. Maybe. *(John heads upstairs. Gregory looks at his watch and begins to chop onions. Buzz covers his eyes with some computer printouts and rests. John waits upstairs while Ramon sits downstairs. Arthur, Perry, and Bobby come into view. They are driving in heavy traffic.)*

PERRY. Cunt! Goddamn cunt. Fuck you and your ultimate driving machine!

ARTHUR. Perry!

PERRY. Well, they *are* when they drive like that.

ARTHUR. Don't use that word.

PERRY. Men are cunts when they drive like that. Did you see how she just cut right in front of me?

BOBBY. Are you talking to me? Sorry, I was reading the life of Ray Charles. What happened?

PERRY. Some asshole-whore-cunt-bitch-dyke with New Jersey license plates and Republican candidates on her bumper practically took my fender off at seventy miles an hour.

BOBBY. It sounds like an extremely cunt-like maneuver, Batman.

PERRY. You see? Boy Wonder agree with Bruce.

ARTHUR. I think you're both disgusting. If I had any convictions I'd ask you to let me out right here.

PERRY. You have too many convictions. That's your trouble.

ARTHUR. Maybe you have too few and that's yours.

PERRY. They're just words. They don't mean anything.

ARTHUR. Can I quote him, Batboy?

PERRY. I was mad. Words only mean something if you say them when you're not mad and mean them. I agree: "Nancy Reagan is a cunt" is an offensive remark.

BOBBY. I wouldn't go that far, Bruce.

PERRY. But "Cunt!" when she grabs a cab in front of you after you've been waiting twenty minutes on a rainy night and she just pops out from Lutèce is a justifiable emotional response to an enormous social injustice.

BOBBY. You're right. He's right. Let's all kill ourselves.

ARTHUR. All I'm saying is, it's never right to use words to hurt another person.

PERRY. How did I hurt her? She didn't hear me. She's halfway to Poughkeepsie by now, the bitch. Don't get me started again. I was just calming down.

ARTHUR. We hurt ourselves when we use them. We're all diminished.

PERRY. You're right. I don't agree with you, but you're right.

ARTHUR. Of course I'm right, you big fairy. And what are you laughing at back there, you visual gimp? There's no really good insulting word for a blind person, is there?

BOBBY. I think you people decided nature had done enough to us and declared a moratorium.

PERRY. Do you ever wonder what Gregory looks like?

ARTHUR. Perry!

BOBBY. It's all right. I don't mind. I know what he looks like.

PERRY. No, I mean, what he really looks like.

BOBBY. I know what he really looks like. He's handsome. His eyes shine. He has wonderful blond hair.

PERRY. But you've never seen blond hair. You have no concept of it.

BOBBY. In my mind's eye, I do, Horatio.

ARTHUR. That shut you up.

BOBBY. That wasn't my intention. In my mind's eye, I see very clearly the same things you and Perry take for granted. Gregory's heart is beautiful.

PERRY. What do we look like?

ARTHUR. Perry!

BOBBY. Like bookends.

PERRY. Is that a compliment?

BOBBY. I think you've come to look more and more like each other over the years.

PERRY. You haven't known us that long.

ARTHUR. That's not what he's saying.

BOBBY. I think you love each other very much. I think you'll stick it out, whatever. I think right now you're holding hands — that when Perry has to take his hand from yours, Arthur, to steer in traffic, he puts it back in yours as soon as he can. I think this is how you always drive. I think this is how you go through life.

ARTHUR. Don't stop.

BOBBY. I think you're both wearing light blue Calvin Klein shirts and chinos.

PERRY. Wrong!

ARTHUR. Look out for that car — !

PERRY. I see it, I see it! What color is my hair?

BOBBY. What hair? You're totally bald.

PERRY. Wrong again. What color?

BOBBY. I wanted to be wrong. I don't like this game. It's making me afraid.

RAMON. Okay. *(He stands up.)*

JOHN. He's coming. *(Ramon starts up to John's room.)*

PERRY. I'm sorry. I didn't ... *(They drive in silence. Ramon comes into the bedroom. John is sitting on the bed.)*

JOHN. Hello.

RAMON. Hi.

JOHN. I'm sorry.

RAMON. Look, I'm sort of out of my element this weekend. He's Gregory Mitchell, for Christ's sake. Do you know what that means? You're all old friends. You work together. You have a company. I'm just somebody you brought with you. I'd appreciate a little more respect, okay? I'm being honest.

JOHN. Okay.

RAMON. Thank you. What's wrong with your neck?

JOHN. Would you be an angel and massage my shoulders?

27

RAMON.   Sure. Just show me where. *(Ramon works on John.)*
BOBBY.   Now it's my turn. I want you to tell me what someone looks like.
PERRY.   Don't tell me, let me guess: Tom Cruise, Willard Scott. I give up, who?
BOBBY.   John.
ARTHUR.   John Jeckyll?
BOBBY.   What does he look like? Describe him. After all this time, I still can't get a picture.
PERRY.   Can you visualize Satan, Bobby?
ARTHUR.   Don't start.
PERRY.   Do you have a concept of evil?
BOBBY.   A very good one, actually.
ARTHUR.   Not everyone shares your opinion, Perry. Perry has a problem with John, Bobby.
PERRY.   I don't have a problem with him. I can't stand him and I wish he were dead.
JOHN.   Don't stop.
PERRY.   Beware him, Bobby. People like you are too good for this world, so people like John Jeckyll have to destroy them.
ARTHUR.   You can't say these things, Perry.
PERRY.   Yes, I can. He doesn't have to believe them.
BOBBY.   I'm not so good. If anything, this world is too good for us.
PERRY.   What do you care what John Jeckyll looks like anyway?
BOBBY.   I just wondered. People like that intrigue me.
PERRY.   What? Shits?
ARTHUR.   It's going to be a wonderful weekend.
PERRY.   What does that mean?
ARTHUR.   John had nowhere to go, so Gregory invited him.
BOBBY.   Didn't Gregory tell you?
PERRY.   No, he did not. Probably because he knew I wouldn't come if he did. Shit! Why would Greg do this to me?
ARTHUR.   He didn't. He told me. I elected not to tell you.
PERRY.   Why?
ARTHUR.   "Why?"!

PERRY. I assume he's coming alone.

ARTHUR. Why would you assume that?

PERRY. Who would willingly spend Memorial Day weekend at a wonderful big house in the country on a gorgeous lake with John Jeckyll when they could be suffocating in the city all by themselves?

BOBBY. He's bringing someone.

ARTHUR. A new boyfriend?

PERRY. One of the Menendez brothers.

BOBBY. A dancer.

ARTHUR. Someone from the company?

BOBBY. No. I think Greg said his name was Ramon. Ramon Something.

ARTHUR. Sounds Latino.

PERRY. "Something" sounds Latino? Since when?

BOBBY. He's Puerto Rican.

PERRY. A Third World boyfriend. So John Jeckyll has gone PC.

ARTHUR. I don't think Puerto Rico qualifies as Third World.

PERRY. This is like Adolf Hitler shtupping Anne Frank.

ARTHUR. You are really over the top this afternoon!

PERRY. Wait till the weekend's over! Here's the driveway. You're home, Bobby. *(Sounds of the car approaching. Everyone in the house reacts to the sound of it.)*

GREGORY. They're here! Buzz, John! They're here! I hear the car!

PERRY. Any other surprises for us, Bobby?

JOHN. I guess they're here. Perry and Arthur are lovers. Bobby is Greg's.

RAMON. I'm terrible with names.

GREGORY. Buzz, wake up, they're here!

BUZZ. I was dreaming about a vacuum cleaner. I need to get laid. *(Gregory, Buzz, John and Ramon go to greet the others, who are carrying bags.)*

GREGORY. I was beginning to. Um. Worry. How was the. Um. Traffic?

PERRY. Terrible. Especially before Hawthorne Circle.

ARTHUR.   I told him to take the Thruway, but no!

BUZZ.   The train was horrendous. I should have waited for you. But guess who I saw? Tony Leigh and Kyle. Together again. A handshake? What is this shit? I want a hug, Martha.

GREGORY.   Where's my. Um. Angel?

BOBBY.   Hi. Have you been working?

GREGORY.   I didn't leave. Um. The studio. Um. All week.

BOBBY.   How did it go?

GREGORY.   Great. Don't ask. Terrible. *(They embrace and withdraw a little.)*

JOHN.   Hello, Perry. Arthur. You both look terrific. Don't you two put on weight? Ever? Anywhere?

ARTHUR.   Look who's talking! I'd love to see the portrait in his closet.

JOHN.   No, you wouldn't. Ramon, Arthur and Perry.

PERRY.   He's Arthur, I'm Perry. He's nice, I'm not. Hi.

ARTHUR.   We're both nice. Don't listen to him.

BUZZ.   So what are you driving now, boys? A Ford Taurus?

PERRY.   What do you care, you big fruit? I don't know. I just get in, turn the key, and go. When they stop, I get a new one.

JOHN.   You should see the wreck we rented.

ARTHUR.   It's a Mazda 626, Buzz.

PERRY.   He's so butch.

ARTHUR.   Someone had to do it. That's why he married me. Can you change a tire?

PERRY.   No.

ARTHUR.   Neither can I.

BUZZ.   That's from *Annie Get Your Gun.* "Can you bake a pie?" "No." "Neither can I." Ethel Merman was gay, you know. So was Irving Berlin. I don't think English is Ramon's first language.

GREGORY.   I missed you.

BOBBY.   It's so good to be here. The city is awful. You can't breathe. They still haven't fixed the dryer. Flor was in hysterics. Here. I've got your mail in my backpack.

GREGORY.   What's this?

BOBBY.   The CDs you wanted. And I got your sheet music

from Patelson's.

GREGORY.   You didn't have to.

BOBBY.   I wanted to.

GREGORY.   John, look, the Elliott Carter!

RAMON.   *(To Bobby.)* Hi, I'm Ramon.

GREGORY.   I'm sorry! *(Ramon puts his hand out to Bobby.)* Bobby doesn't. Um. See, Ramon.

RAMON.   I'm sorry. I didn't —

BOBBY.   Don't be sorry. Just come here! *(He hugs Ramon.)* Welcome. Ramon, is it?

RAMON.   Right.

BOBBY.   Latino?

RAMON.   Yes.

BOBBY.   *Mi casa es su casa.* I bet you were wishing I wasn't going to say that.

BUZZ.   We all were, Bobby.

PERRY, ARTHUR and BUZZ.   We all were!

RAMON.   Listen, that's about as much Spanish as I speak.

BOBBY.   You're kidding.

RAMON.   Sorry to disappoint you. The Commonwealth of Puerto Rico is a territory of U.S. imperialism.

JOHN.   No speeches, please, Ramon. No one's interested.

RAMON.   We speak American. We think American. We dress American. The only thing we don't do is move or make love American.

BOBBY.   I've been like this since birth, Ramon. Gregory and I have been together four years. I get around fine. It'll surprise you. Any more questions?

RAMON.   *(Off guard.)* No. *(They separate.)*

GREGORY.   Let me. Um. Show you. Um. To your room.

ARTHUR.   After all these years, I think we know, Gregory. If those walls could talk!

BUZZ.   They don't have to. We've all heard you.

ARTHUR.   What room are you in?

BUZZ.   That little horror under the eaves. I call it the Patty Hearst Memorial Closet.

ARTHUR.   Give me a hand with these, will you, Perry?

PERRY.   I told you not to take so much.

ARTHUR. It's my hair dryer.

PERRY. You don't have enough hair to justify an appliance that size.

ARTHUR. Has it ever occurred to you that I stopped listening to you at least ten years ago?

RAMON. Here, let me.

ARTHUR. Thank you. *(They will start moving to the house.)*

GREGORY. We're having. Um. *Salade Nicoise.* Um. For lunch.

BUZZ. You know I'm allergic to anchovies.

GREGORY. We just. Um. Swam the float out. Me. Um. And Ramon.

BUZZ. He knows I'm allergic to anchovies.

PERRY. I'm not going in that lake until you get it heated.

GREGORY. I hope you brought. Um. Your swimsuits.

ARTHUR. No one is wearing swimsuits. We're all going skinny-dipping after lunch. What are we? Men or wimps?

BUZZ. You just want to see everyone's dick.

ARTHUR. I've seen everyone's dick. Answer the question.

BUZZ. Sometimes we're men and sometimes we're wimps. You haven't seen Ramon's dick.

ARTHUR. You're a troublemaker.

BUZZ. I'm not a troublemaker. I'm an imp. A gay imp. *(He goes. The new arrivals are beginning to settle in. Perry and John remain for the following until indicated.)*

PERRY. Anyway. Gregory knew he'd left Bobby downstairs and outside the house.

GREGORY. Does everyone. Um. Have towels?

PERRY. It was their ritual. Whenever they arrived at the house from the city, Bobby liked to be alone outside for a while, even in winter. Gregory never asked what he did.

BOBBY. Hello, house.

ARTHUR. Greg! We need some towels.

PERRY. No, we don't. We brought our own. Remember?

BOBBY. Hello, trees.

ARTHUR. Never mind! That's right, we hate his towels.

BOBBY. Hello, lake.

GREGORY. Who said they needed towels?

PERRY. Greg's house is very large.

ARTHUR.   Too large. I get sick of shouting. We're fine! Forget the towels!

BOBBY.   I bless you all.

PERRY.   None of us saw Ramon when he returned to the
driveway, the parked cars, and Bobby. Arthur and I were set-
tling in. *(Ramon has returned to where Bobby is standing. He
watches him.)*

JOHN.   I was on the phone to London with my brother,
James.

PERRY.   I didn't know you had a brother.

JOHN.   A twin brother. We're like *that. (He opens his arms
wide.)* He's not well.

PERRY.   I'm sorry.

JOHN.   This is about them. *(He nods toward Bobby and
Ramon.)*

PERRY.   Minutes passed. Gregory fussed. Buzz washed salad
greens in his hosts' pricey balsamic vinegar. He's very diligent
about germs. He has to be. Ramon looked at Bobby.

BOBBY.   Thank you, God.

RAMON.   Excuse me?

BOBBY.   Who's that?

RAMON.   I'm sorry.

BOBBY.   You startled me.

RAMON.   It's Ramon. I'm sorry. I thought you said something.

BOBBY.   I was thanking God for all this. The trees, the lake,
the sweet, sweet air. For being here. For all of us together in
Gregory's house.

RAMON.   I didn't mean to interrupt or anything.

BOBBY.   I'm not crazy. I'm happy.

RAMON.   I understand.

GREGORY.   Here are the towels you asked for.

ARTHUR.   Thank you.

GREGORY.   Anything else?

ARTHUR.   We're fine.

GREGORY.   Perry?

PERRY.   We're fine.

GREGORY.   Um. I'm glad. Um. You're both here.

RAMON.   Do you need a hand with anything?

BOBBY.   No, thanks.

BUZZ.   Pssst! Gregory!

GREGORY.   What?

BUZZ.   John is on the phone to his brother in London. I didn't hear him use a credit card or reverse the charges.

GREGORY.   Um. I'm sure he'll. Um. Tell me.

BUZZ.   Don't you ever believe the worst about anyone?

GREGORY.   No. *(Ramon hasn't moved. He scarcely breathes. He has not taken his eyes off Bobby.)*

BOBBY.   You're still there, aren't you? What are you doing? What do you want? Don't be afraid. Tell me. All right. Don't. Stay there. I'll come to you. Just tell me, should I fall (which I don't plan to), what color are my trousers? I think I put on white. I hope so. It's Memorial Day.

PERRY.   I don't know why, but I'm finding this very painful.

BOBBY.   Children play at this and call it Blindman's Bluff. Imagine your whole life being a children's birthday-party game!

JOHN.   Painful, erotic, and absurd.

BOBBY.   I can feel you. I can hear you. I'm getting warm. I'm getting close. I like this game. I'm very good at it. I'm going to win. You haven't got a chance.

PERRY.   Bobby didn't see the rake. *(Bobby trips and falls. He hurts himself. There will be a gash on his forehead.)*

RAMON.   Oh!

BOBBY.   He speaks! The cat has let go his tongue. I wouldn't say no to a hand. *(Ramon goes. Bobby calls after him.)* At least tell me, what color are my trousers?

PERRY.   *(Moved.)* White. White.

BOBBY.   Sometimes I get tired of behaving like a grown-up. Ow! Gregory! *(At once, everyone converges on the scene and surrounds him.)*

GREGORY.   What happened?

BOBBY.   I'm okay. Just —

GREGORY.   The rake! You tripped. It's my fault. Um.

PERRY.   Take his other arm.

BOBBY.   I'm fine. I want Gregory to do it.

BUZZ.   Who would leave a rake out like that?

ARTHUR.   Shut up, will you?

JOHN.   He's cut.

BOBBY.   I'm not cut.

JOHN.   His forehead.

BOBBY.   What color are my trousers?

GREGORY.   White.

BOBBY.   Are there grass stains on them?

BUZZ.   Bobby, you are the only fairy in America who still wears white pants on the first holiday of summer.

BOBBY.   I was hoping I was the only person in America who still wears white pants on the first holiday of summer.

PERRY.   White pants were before my time even, and I'm pushing forty.

BUZZ.   Not. You pushed forty when *Chorus Line* was still running.

PERRY.   That's not true. I was born in 19 —

ARTHUR.   We have an injured person here. *(Ramon returns.)*

BOBBY.   I'm not injured.

JOHN.   Where have you been?

RAMON.   Down by the lake. What happened?

BOBBY.   Nothing happened. Who's that?

BUZZ.   The new kid on the block.

RAMON.   Is he all right?

BOBBY.   I fell. Big deal. I do it all the time.

GREGORY.   No, you don't. No, he doesn't.

BOBBY.   Now everyone back off. Everyone but Gregory. I can feel you all crowding around me.

GREGORY.   One!

BOBBY.   What are you doing?

BUZZ.   Rhett picks up Scarlett and carries her up the stairs.

GREGORY.   Two!

BOBBY.   No, I don't want you to.

GREGORY.   Three! *(He tries to pick Bobby up but can't. He staggers with the weight, then sets him down. The others look away in embarrassment.)* I couldn't get a good. Um. Grip.

BOBBY.   It's not you. It's all that ice cream I've been eating.

GREGORY.   That's never happened. Usually I — I feel so —

BOBBY. It's okay, it's okay. *(Bobby and Gregory go into the house. The others hang behind somewhat sheepishly.)*
BUZZ. *(Singing.)* "Just a weekend in the country."
RAMON. Is that a joke?
BUZZ. Come on, I need you in the kitchen. I'll explain the entire Sondheim oeuvre to you while we peel potatoes. I'm borrowing your humpy boyfriend, John. I love the way I said that. Oeuvre. I'm quite impressed. Oeuvre. Say it with me. Oeuvre. *(Buzz and Ramon go.)*
ARTHUR. Don't ever try to pick me up.
PERRY. It's lucky for you I did.
JOHN. I'd rung off from my brother feeling a rage and a desolation I didn't know how to cope with. "Didn't"? I never have.
ARTHUR. What's the matter?
JOHN. My twin brother. The National Theatre seamstress. He wants to come over. He's not well. He needs me and I don't like him.
ARTHUR. That's a tough order. I don't envy you. Perry, I'm going to take a canoe out. You want to come?
PERRY. I promised Greg I'd go over some company business with him.
ARTHUR. It's your last chance to get rid of me.
PERRY. No, it's not. *(Arthur goes. Only Perry and John remain.)* I work with quite a few AIDS organizations.
JOHN. Thank you.
PERRY. They can help him find a doctor.
JOHN. Thank you.
PERRY. It never ends.
JOHN. No.
PERRY. How does Buzz look to you?
JOHN. I don't know. How does he look to you?
PERRY. I can't tell anymore.
JOHN. He wouldn't tell me if things were worse.
PERRY. I can't look at him sometimes.
JOHN. Anyway.
PERRY. *(Pleasantly.)* You got that from me, you know.
JOHN. Got what?

PERRY. The "anyway."

JOHN. It's a word in the dictionary. Page 249. You can't copyright the English language, duck.

PERRY. Hey, I'm trying! Fuck you. *(He goes.)*

JOHN. Anyway. *En tout cas!* The weekend had begun. Everyone was in place. Old wounds reopened. New alliances forged. For fifteen minutes, while I helped Arthur wash their car, he was my best friend in the entire world. Later that afternoon, after too much picnic, when I came upon him and Perry all cozy in a hammock on the porch, he barely gave me the time of day. The hours until dinner seemed endless. *(The other men are reassembling for after-dinner after a very big meal.)*

PERRY. No, Gregory. It's out of the question. Jesus, I hope this isn't why you invited us out here for the weekend.

GREGORY. I've. Um. Committed us.

PERRY. Well *un*commit us!

GREGORY. It's too late.

PERRY. Leave it to me. I'll get you out of it.

GREGORY. No, I want to. Um. Do it. It's for a good cause.

PERRY. I don't care if it's the greatest cause in the history of Western civilization, which it's not, you are not going to find six men, nondancers all, to put on tutus and do *Swan Lake* for another AIDS benefit at Carnegie Hall. You're not going to find one man!

BUZZ. Speak for yourself, Perry.

PERRY. Well, *you!* The love child of Judy Garland and Liberace.

ARTHUR. When is it, Greg?

GREGORY. Um. It's. Um. Early September, right after Labor Day.

PERRY. Bobby, tell your lover he is not going to find six men to make fools of themselves like that.

BOBBY. How would they be making fools of themselves?

PERRY. By dressing like women. Men in drag turn my stomach.

RAMON. Why?

ARTHUR. Don't start, Perry.

BUZZ. You wouldn't be in drag. I'd have you in tulle, lots

37

and lots of tulle. A vision of hairy legs in a tutu and toe shoes.

PERRY.   This will go over big at the NEA, Gregory. That's all we need. A picture of you looking like some flaming fairy in the Arts and Leisure section.

GREGORY.   I. Um. I am a flaming fairy. I thought we all were.

PERRY.   You know what I'm talking about.

BOBBY.   Don't yell at him. It was my idea I thought it would be funny.

PERRY.   What do you know about funny? I'm sorry, Bobby, but sometimes boyfriends should stay boyfriends.

GREGORY.   Sometimes. Um. Lawyers should stay. Um. Lawyers.

PERRY.   You've done enough for AIDS. We all have.

GREGORY.   Nobody's done enough. Um. For AIDS.

BOBBY.   It's okay, Gregory.

GREGORY.   Never mind, Perry. I'll ask someone else. Now who wants what?

ARTHUR.   We're all fine.

PERRY.   No, we're not.

JOHN.   People are bloody sick of benefits, Gregory.

PERRY.   That's the truth.

BUZZ.   Not the people they're being given for.

GREGORY.   *Basta,* Buzz. The subject is closed.

ARTHUR.   Dinner was delicious. The mashed potatoes were fabulous, Gregory.

BUZZ.   The mashed potatoes were mine. *(He sings from* The King and I.*)* I don't know why I've bothered to perfect a flawless imitation of Gertrude Lawrence when none of you cretins has even heard of her!

JOHN.   We've heard, luv. We don't care.

BOBBY.   Who's Gertrude Lawrence?

PERRY.   A British actress.

* See Special Note on Songs and Recordings on copyright page.

GREGORY.   She was. Um. Gay, you know.

BUZZ.   That's not funny. Julie Andrews made a rotten film about her.

ARTHUR.   Isn't Julie Andrews gay?

BUZZ.   I don't know. She never fucked me. Don't interrupt. Gertrude Lawrence wasn't an actress. She was a star. Hence, the rotten film, *Star!*, but don't get me started on movies. Movies are for people who have to eat popcorn while they're being entertained. Next question? Yes, you, at the end of the table with the lindenberry sorbét all over his face.

RAMON.   Who's Julie Andrews?

BUZZ.   I should have seen that one coming. I was born in the wrong decade, that's my problem.

RAMON.   I was kidding. I saw *Mary Poppins*. But who's Liberace?

BOBBY.   Who's Judy Garland? Who are any of those people? *(Bobby and Ramon laugh together.)*

ARTHUR.   You want me to clear up, Gregory?

BUZZ.   Who's Ethel Merman? Who's Mary Martin? Who's Beatrice Lillie? Who's anybody? We're all going to be dead and forgotten anyway.

BOBBY.   Gregory's not.

BUZZ.   I'm talking about mattering!

PERRY.   I just don't want to be dead and forgotten in my own lifetime.

ARTHUR.   Nattering?

BUZZ.   Mattering! Really mattering.

ARTHUR.   Oh, I thought you said "nattering"!

JOHN.   You admit people like Gertrude Lawrence don't really matter?

ARTHUR.   I thought he said "nattering."

BUZZ.   I cannot believe a subject of the U.K. could make a remark like that. Gertrude Lawrence brought pleasure to hundreds of thousands of people. You wrote a musical that ran for eleven performances.

JOHN.   I have United States citizenship.

RAMON.   I know who Barbra Streisand is.

BUZZ.   She'll be very pleased to hear that.

BOBBY.   I don't know who most of those people are, either.

PERRY.   When did you take out U.S. citizenship?

JOHN.   Nine years ago. October 25.

BUZZ.   Barbara Cook's birthday. "Who's Barbara Cook?" No one. Nobody. Forget it. Die listening to your Madonna albums. I long for the day when people ask "Who's Madonna?" I apologize to the teenagers at the table, but the state of the American musical has me very upset.

PERRY.   The state of America is what should get you upset.

BUZZ.   It does. It's a metaphor, you asshole!

PERRY.   Now just a minute!

BUZZ.   I have a picture of a starving child in Somalia over my desk at the clinic. He's covered in dust.

JOHN.   We all know the picture.

PERRY.   It doesn't justify you calling me an asshole.

BUZZ.   The child has fallen forward on his haunches, he's so weak from hunger, he can barely lift his head.

PERRY.   Buzz, we know the picture. It was in every magazine and paper.

BUZZ.   Clearly, the kid is dying. He's got what? Five minutes? Ten? Five feet away a vulture sits. Sits and waits. He's not even looking at the kid. He's that confident where his next meal is coming from. There's no way this kid is going to jump up and launch into a number from *Oliver!* or *Porgy and Bess.*

PERRY.   We've all seen the picture!

BOBBY.   *(Quietly.)* I haven't. *(Gregory takes his hand.)*

PERRY.   What is your point?

BUZZ.   Point? I don't have a point. Why does everything have to have a point? To make it comfortable? I look at that picture every day and I get sick to my stomach and some days I even cry a little. The newspaper has already yellowed, but the nausea and the occasional tears keep coming. But so what? So fucking what? That kid is dead meat by now.

JOHN.   That's disgusting.

BUZZ.   You bet it is.

JOHN.   Your language.

BUZZ.   So sue me. That's from *Guys and Dolls,* for you

kiddies.

RAMON. Happy Memorial Day.

PERRY. I think the point is, we're all sitting around here talking about something, pretending to care.

ARTHUR. No one's pretending.

PERRY. Pretending to care, when the truth is there's nothing we can do about it. It would hurt too much to really care. You wouldn't have a stomach ache, you'd be dead from the dry heaves from throwing your guts up for the rest of your life. That kid is a picture in a newspaper who makes us feel bad for having it so good. But feed him, brush him off, and in ten years he's just another nigger to scare the shit out of us. Apologies tendered, but that's how I see it.

ARTHUR. Apologies not accepted.

GREGORY. Don't, you two.

ARTHUR. I hate it when he talks like that.

PERRY. You'd rather I dissembled, sirrah? (I wasn't an English major at Williams for nothing!)

ARTHUR. Yes. I'd rather you would. Rather the man I shared my life with and loved with all my heart, rather he dissembled than let me see the hate and bile there.

PERRY. The hate and bile aren't for you, love.

ARTHUR. That's not good enough, Perry. After a while, the hate and bile are for everyone. It all comes around. (He starts clearing the table.)

PERRY. Anyway.

ARTHUR. I hate that word. You use it to get yourself out of every tight corner you've ever found yourself in. Shall I load the washer?

GREGORY. Just rinse and stack. Thank you, Arthur.

RAMON. Do you need a hand?

ARTHUR. No, thank you. (He goes.)

PERRY. The younger generation hasn't put in their two cents, I notice.

RAMON. As a person of color, I think you're full of shit. As a gay man, I think —

JOHN. No one cares what you think as a gay man, duck. That wasn't the question. What do you think as a member of the human race?

RAMON.   As a gay man, I think you're full of shit. *(We hear a door slam. Arthur isn't back. Everyone reacts.)* I think the problem begins right here, the way we relate to one another as gay men.

JOHN.   This is tired, Ramon. Very, very tired.

RAMON.   I don't think it is. We don't love one another because we don't love ourselves.

JOHN.   Clichés! Clichés!

RAMON.   Where is the love at this table? I want to see the love at this table.

BOBBY.   I love Gregory.

GREGORY.   I love Bobby.

PERRY.   I love Arthur. I love Gregory. I love Bobby. I love Buzz. Right now I love you, your righteous anger.

BUZZ.   I sure as hell don't love anyone at this table right now. All right, Bobby and Greg. A little bit, but only because they're our hosts.

JOHN.   I love the Queen; she's been through hell lately. My Aunt Olivia in Brighton in a pensioners' villa — old-age home, you call them? My Welsh Corgi, Dylan, even though he's been dead lo these eleven years (I'm surprised his name came up!). And my job.

GREGORY.   Thank you.

RAMON.   Everything you love is dead or old or inanimal. Don't you love anything that's alive and new?

JOHN.   Of course I do, but I choose not to share them around a dinner table. And you mean "inanimate."

PERRY.   That's honest.

JOHN.   I thought that's what we were all being. Otherwise, what's the point? Are you satisfied, Ramon?

RAMON.   None of you said yourself.

PERRY.   Maybe it goes without saying.

JOHN.   We were waiting for you, Ramon. How do you love yourself? Let us count the ways.

RAMON.   I love myself. I love myself when I dance.

JOHN.   That's one.

RAMON.   I love myself when I'm dancing. When I feel the

42

music right here. When I'm moving in time and space. Gregory knows what I'm talking about.

GREGORY. Yes, yes, I do.

RAMON. When I dance I become all the best things I can be.

JOHN. Ramon loves himself when he dances. That's still only one, Chiquita. One and counting.

RAMON. I love myself when I'm making love with a really hot man. I love myself when I'm eating really good food. I love myself when I'm swimming naked.

JOHN. That's four.

RAMON. The rest of the time I just feel okay.

PERRY. I'm jealous. We don't reach such an apotheosis at the law firm of Cohen, Mendelssohn and Leibowitz.

RAMON. But most of all I love myself when I'm dancing well and no one can touch me.

JOHN. Is this as a gay dancer, luv?

RAMON. Fuck you, John.

BUZZ. You tell him, sweetheart. That's right: Fuck you, John.

JOHN. Americans use that expression entirely too often.

BUZZ. Everybody!

ALL BUT JOHN. Fuck you, John!

JOHN. In England we think it nearly as often as you do, but we don't actually say it to someone's face. It would be too rude. Half the people who are being knighted at the Palace every year are thinking "Fuck you" as they're being tapped with that little sword, but they don't come right out and say it, the way an American would, which is why we don't knight Americans, the only reason—you're too uncouth.

ALL BUT JOHN. Fuck you.

JOHN. What do you mean when you tell another person "Fuck you"?

RAMON. Fuck you, John. And don't you ever call me Chiquita again.

BUZZ. This is good.

JOHN. I think you mean several things. Mixed signals, I believe they're called in therapeutic circles. "I hate you. Get out of my life." At least, "I hate you, get out of my life for the moment."

RAMON.   Fuck you.

JOHN.   "I love you, but you don't love me. I want to kill you, but I can't so I will hurt you instead. I want to make you feel small and insignificant, the way you've made me feel. I want to make you feel every terrible thing my entire life right up until this moment has made me feel." Ah, there's the link! I knew we'd find it. The common bond uniting this limey and the Yanks. The resolution of our fraternal theme.

RAMON.   I said "Fuck you."

JOHN.   But until we recognize and accept this mutual "Fuck you" in each of us, with every last fiber of my fading British being, every last ounce of my tobaccoed English breath, I say "Fuck you" right back. Fuck you, Ramon. Fuck you, Buzz. Fuck you, Perry. Fuck you, Gregory. Fuck you, Bobby. Fuck all of you. Well, I think I've said my piece. *(He moves away from the others, who remain at the table.)* I feel like playing, Gregory. Did you have your mighty Bechstein tuned in honor of our royal visit?

GREGORY.   The man. Um. Was just here.

JOHN.   What would you like to hear?

PERRY.   I don't think anyone much cares.

JOHN.   I'll play very softly.

BUZZ.   I don't suppose you know *Subways Are for Sleeping?*

JOHN.   Would anyone say no to a little Chopin?

RAMON.   I would.

JOHN.   One of the nocturnes. *(He goes into the next room.)*

RAMON.   I'm still saying "Fuck you," John!

BUZZ.   What brought that on?

PERRY.   His brother?

BUZZ.   That's no excuse. Play something gay. We want gay music written by a gay composer.

PERRY.   There's no such thing as gay music, Buzz.

BUZZ.   Well, maybe there should be. I'm sick of straight people. Tell the truth, aren't you? There's too goddamn many of them. I was in the bank yesterday. They were everywhere. Writing checks, making deposits. Two of them were applying for a mortgage. It was disgusting. They're taking over. No one wants to talk about it, but it's true. *(John starts playing the piano, off.)*

JOHN.   *(Off.)* This is for you, Buzz. It's by Tchaikovsky. Peter Ilitch. One of us. Can't you tell? All these dominant triads are so, so gay! Who did he think he was fooling, writing music like this? *(Melancholy music fills the room. They listen.)*

BUZZ.   I like this. It's not Jerry Herman, but it's got a beat. *(Perry gets up.)*

GREGORY.   Where. Um...?

PERRY.   I'd better find Arthur. *(He goes.)*

JOHN.   *(Off.)* This is depressing. How's this, Gregory? *(He starts playing the* Dance of the Little Swans *from* Swan Lake.*)*

BUZZ.   That's more like it.

GREGORY.   That's the. Um. Music. *Swan Lake.* The benefit. The *Pas des Cygnes.* Thank you, John. *(Gregory stands up from the table. He begins to dance the* Pas des Cygnes *from* Swan Lake. *He is an entirely different person when he moves: free, spontaneous, as physically fluent as he is verbally inhibited.)*

BUZZ.   What are you doing?

GREGORY.   The *Pas de Cygnes.*

BUZZ.   I don't do *Pas de Cygnes.* What is it?

GREGORY.   The *Dance of the Swans.* Come on. I can't do it alone. Ramon!

RAMON.   No, thanks.

GREGORY.   Come on, Buzz!

BUZZ.   Why are you holding your arms like that? *(Indeed, as Gregory dances he holds his arms crossed in front of him, each hand on its opposite side, ready to link hands with another person and form a chain.)*

GREGORY.   I'm waiting for you to take my hand.

JOHN.   *(Off.)* What are you doing in there?

GREGORY.   We're dancing! Don't stop! Take my hand, Buzz. *(Buzz tentatively takes his hand and will try to follow Gregory's steps.)*

BOBBY.   What are they doing?

RAMON.   Now they're both dancing.

BOBBY.   How do they look?

BUZZ.   Ridiculous. What do you think?

BOBBY.   You see? I knew it would be funny. *(Ramon and Bobby begin to laugh. Gregory and Buzz continue to dance while John plays the piano from another room.)*
GREGORY.   That's it, Buzz, that's it.
BUZZ.   My admiration for Chita Rivera has just become boundless!
RAMON.   You should see this.
BOBBY.   I can imagine.
JOHN.   Can I stop?
THE OTHERS.   NO!!
GREGORY.   Now you've got it!
BUZZ.   Eat your heart out, Donna McKechnie! *(Their arms linked, Gregory and Buzz dance themselves out of the house and out onto the grounds.)*
BOBBY.   What happened?
RAMON.   They're gone. They danced themselves right out onto the lawn. *(Perry has joined Arthur down by the lake.)*
PERRY.   Listen to them up there. We're missing all the fun.
ARTHUR.   We better talk.
PERRY.   Okay. I brought you a sweater.
ARTHUR.   Thank you.
PERRY.   And one of their blankets. I thought we could spread it and look at the sky. The stars are incredible. Thick as ... whatever stars are thick as. "Molasses" doesn't sound right.
ARTHUR.   Thieves? No. Diamonds! Thick as diamonds on a jeweler's black felt!
PERRY.   I love you.
ARTHUR.   I know. Me, too.
PERRY.   I'm sorry we don't always understand each other. I hate it when we're not in sync. I hate what I said at the table.
ARTHUR.   I hated it, too.
PERRY.   I just get so frightened sometimes, so angry.
ARTHUR.   It's all right, Perry, we all do.
PERRY.   Don't give up on me.
ARTHUR.   No. I thought you were coming down here with me. It's spectacular. I can see Orion's Belt and both Dippers.
PERRY.   That's not the Dipper. That's the Dipper. *(The pi-*

ano music stops. John comes back into the room where Bobby and Ramon are.)

JOHN. Where is everyone?

BOBBY. They were last sighted heading for the boathouse. Gregory was very pleased with himself.

JOHN. You see, I'm good for something. I'm not entirely bad!

BOBBY. No one is, John.

JOHN. Thank you. I can't tell you how good that makes me feel. I was a shit tonight and I'm not even drunk. I'm sorry, Ramon. Am I forgiven?

BOBBY. Ramon?

JOHN. "Am I forgiven?" I said.

RAMON. Yes.

JOHN. Thank you. Forgiveness is good. We all need it from time to time. It's this business with my brother. *(He goes back into the adjoining room and begins to play a Beethoven sonata.)*

BOBBY. Are you still there?

RAMON. Yes.

BOBBY. What are you doing?

RAMON. Nothing.

JOHN. *(Off.)* This one is for me.

ARTHUR. He plays beautifully, the son of a bitch. The devil's fingers.

PERRY. So many stars, so many stars! Say a prayer for Buzz.

BUZZ. Arthur and Perry lay on blankets and looked at the heavens and talked things out. Gregory danced on by a couple of times. John played a melancholy piano until the wee small hours of the morning. Bobby and Ramon sat quietly talking across the deserted dining table empty glasses, soiled napkins between them. All in all, there was a lot of love in Gregory and Bobby's house that first night of the first holiday weekend of the summer. It didn't start raining till the next morning. It didn't stop until the drive back home on Monday night. It rained all weekend.

BOBBY. It was raining when Buzz started crying in the middle of a movie on AMC and couldn't stop.

RAMON. It was raining when Gregory sat alone in his studio for six hours listening to a piece of music and didn't move from his chair.

BUZZ.   It was raining when Ramon waited for Bobby by the refrigerator and he dropped the bottle.

ARTHUR.   It was raining when John wanted Ramon to fuck him the next afternoon anyway.

PERRY.   Anyway! There's that word again. And he's wrong, this one. I don't say "anyway" when I'm cornered. I say it when I'm overcome. I love you, Arthur Pape. *(He kisses Arthur on the lips. Gregory and Buzz will dance by again. They are having a wonderful time. Bobby and Ramon remain at the dining table. John is playing a Chopin nocturne. The lights fade. The music swells.)*

ACT TWO

Lakeside. Blaze of noon.

The men are singing "In the Good Old Summertime."

As they move apart, they reveal Ramon sprawled naked on an old-fashioned wooden float at a distance offshore.

One by one, they stop singing, turn around, and take a long look back at Ramon splayed on the raft.

Even Bobby.

Finally, only John and Ramon remain.

JOHN. Anyway. *(He turns away from Ramon and takes out Gregory's journal and begins to read.)* "Fourth of July weekend. Manderley. Promise of good weather. After Memorial Day we deserve it. John Jeckyll is arriving with his twin brother, James. Perry has already dubbed them James the Fair and John the Foul. John will also have Ramon Fornos, a superb young dancer, in tow. I thought they were over. Chances of finishing the first section of the new piece before they all descend on us looking slim. Bobby says he will stand sentry outside the studio while I work. I tried to tell him our guests aren't the reason I — Too late. They're here." *(Lights up on Perry, Arthur, Gregory, and Buzz making ready to play tennis doubles. Arthur and Gregory are partners. So are Buzz and Perry. John is free to walk among them as he reads.)*
BUZZ. Which end of the racquet do I hold?
PERRY. That's it! Change partners. You show him, Gregory! *(He crosses to Arthur.)*
BUZZ. Good teachers are patient. *(Arthur is looking off to Ramon.)*

PERRY.   What are you looking at out there?

ARTHUR.   Nothing. *(Gregory has his arms around Buzz in the classic "teacher's" position.)*

GREGORY.   Here, Buzz. Make a. Um. V with your thumb. Um. And forefinger.

BUZZ.   Thank you. See how I respond to human kindness?

GREGORY.   You bring your arm back like this, step into the ball, and pow! *(They continue.)*

JOHN.   "Buzz arrived alone again. We were hoping he'd bring someone. He looks thinner."

PERRY.   Try to keep your eye on this ball, not those.

JOHN.   "Perry and Arthur asked if the could celebrate their anniversary with us. I warned them John would be here."

ARTHUR.   That wasn't called for.

JOHN.   "Poor John. People don't like him." *(He closes the journal and becomes "visible" to the others.)*

PERRY.   I don't want to fight. I want to beat them in tennis.

JOHN.   Who's winning?

BUZZ.   We are. We're killing them.

JOHN.   I can't believe it.

PERRY.   You can't believe it?

BUZZ.   Look who I have for a coach and partner. Why can't you have a twin brother?

ARTHUR.   Don't make Gregory blush!

JOHN.   What's wrong with mine?

BUZZ.   He looks too much like you and acts too much like me. Where are all the men? There are no eligible men!

PERRY.   Will you keep your voice down?

BUZZ.   For what? We're in the middle of nowhere! Will I keep my voice down! You're a martyr, Arthur, a genuine martyr. I would have pushed him off your tasteful lower Fifth Avenue balcony ten years ago.

JOHN.   Ramon is eligible, gentlemen.

BUZZ.   I don't date dancers. I've made it a rule. It's very simple. Dancers don't want to date me. So fuck 'em.

JOHN.   In Ramon's case, you don't know what you're missing. Does anyone want anything from the house?

GREGORY.   There's tea in the. Um. Fridge.

JOHN.   I'll send James down with it. *(He goes.)*
PERRY.   I've got another one: the Princes of Light and Darkness.
ARTHUR.   Could we concentrate on winning this set?
BUZZ.   So what's the score? A thousand to one? I'm really getting into this.
PERRY.   *(Annoyed.)* Love-forty! *(He cranks up for a serve.)*
BUZZ.   Getting ready to serve now, the ever-lovely Dr. Renee Richards. *(Perry flubs.)*
GREGORY.   Double fault. Game! Change sides.
PERRY.   Fuck you, Buzz.
BUZZ.   What did I do? Who won?
GREGORY.   We did.
BUZZ.   We did? We didn't do anything. I love tennis. *(They change sides.)*
PERRY.   You heard John: he's eligible!
ARTHUR.   Perry.
PERRY.   Lighten up. Your serve, Martina. *(The game continues. John is heard playing the piano, off. Ramon raises up and looks around. He shields his eyes with his hand, scans the horizon, and lies back down. Bobby appears. He is wearing a robe. He will advance to the stage apron.)*
BOBBY.   When Gregory told me he thought John and Ramon were over and was surprised that John would be bringing him again, I didn't tell him that they were and that Ramon was coming with him because of me. I didn't tell him that when the phone rang Monday night, and then again Thursday, and there was no one there, and he kept saying "Hello? Hello? Who is this?" I didn't tell him it was Ramon on the other end. *(He falls off the stage.)* Don't anyone touch me. I don't want help. *(He climbs back onto the stage.)* And I didn't tell him what Ramon's mouth felt like against my own. I didn't tell him the last time we made love I thought of it. I didn't tell him Ramon whispered to me this morning. He would be waiting for me on the raft when I swam out there. *(He drops his robe and goes out into the lake. James appears, wheeling a serving cart with iced tea and potato chips.)*
JAMES.   It's not who you think. I'm the other one. When

John stops playing the piano, you can start getting nervous again.

PERRY. Ball!

JAMES. My brother gave me the most extraordinary book. *Outing America: From A to Z.* I'm absolutely riveted.

PERRY. Ball, please!

JAMES. It gives the names of all the gay men and lesbians in this country in alphabetical order, from the pre-Revolutionary period (Pocahontas, I think her name was) right up to now, someone called Dan Rather.

PERRY. Ball, please!

ARTHUR. Which one of them is it?

BUZZ. It must be James. The grass isn't turning brown.

ARTHUR. I think he's attractive, Buzz.

BUZZ. Yeah?

PERRY. Goddamnit! *(Perry retrieves the tennis ball.)* Thanks for nothing.

JAMES. I'm sorry?

PERRY. Just wait till you say, "Ball, please!"

JAMES. I haven't the vaguest notion what you're talking about, luv.

PERRY. Skip it. *(He goes.)*

JAMES. I must say, and I hope you take this in the best possible way, for a young country, you've turned out an awful lot of poufters. In two and a half centuries you've done almost as well as we have in twenty. John Foster Dulles. Who is that? Is it a juicy one? Benjamin Franklin. Him we've heard of. Very into kites. Knute Rockne. Lady Bird Johnson. Americans have the most extraordinary names! Booker T. Washington. Babe Ruth. Buzz Hauser. *(He settles himself to read as Perry rejoins the others.)*

BUZZ. Whose serve is it?

PERRY. Still yours. Don't patronize us.

ARTHUR. We can always stop.

PERRY. No!

BUZZ. What's the matter? Are you okay?

GREGORY. I'm fine. *(He's not. He's tired.)*

BUZZ. Are you sure?

GREGORY. I'm fine!

BUZZ. What's wrong?

GREGORY. I don't. Um. See Bobby.

PERRY. Are we playing or what?

BUZZ. Time. Is that legal? Can I call time?

GREGORY. I saw him go into the lake. Um. He doesn't like me to. Um. Watch him swim. It's an honor. Um. System. And I'm not. Um. Very honorable.

BUZZ. Ramon's out there. He'll be fine.

PERRY. What is the problem, people?

GREGORY. There he is! *(Bobby appears at the side of the raft. He is winded from the swim and just hangs there.)*

BOBBY. Hello? Anyone aboard? *(Ramon doesn't move.)* Ramon? *(Ramon still doesn't move.)*

RAMON. This time I would let him find me. I waited, not daring to breathe, while his hands searched for me on the raft. I prayed to our Holy Blessed Mother I wouldn't get a hard-on.

BOBBY. Ramon?

RAMON. My prayers weren't being answered. I thought I would explode.

BOBBY. Ow! *(He's gotten a splinter from the raft.)*

GREGORY. Ow! *(He's twisted something running for a ball and falls heavily to the ground.)*

BUZZ. Are you hurt?

GREGORY. No. Yes. Ow! *(Buzz, Perry, and Arthur help him to his feet.)* Get some ice.

BUZZ. What is it? Your ankle?

GREGORY. My ankle, my knee, everything.

BUZZ. Careful with him.

PERRY. Take his other arm.

ARTHUR. I've got you. Get him to the house. *(They are helping him off.)*

GREGORY. No, the studio. I've got ice packs there. *(They help him off in another direction. Buzz looks out across the lake to the raft.)*

BUZZ. Bobby! *(Bobby is still hanging on to the raft with one arm. He works on the splinter with his teeth. Ramon sits up and gently*

53

takes hold of Bobby's wrist.)

BOBBY.   Oh! Who's that? *(Ramon takes Bobby's finger, puts it in his mouth, sucks out the splinter, and spits it out.)*

BUZZ.   Bobby! Come in! It's Gregory! He's hurt!

BOBBY.   They're calling me.

RAMON.   I waited for you last night. I thought you'd come down. Meet me somewhere tonight.

BOBBY.   I can't.

RAMON.   I'll be in the garden after supper.

BOBBY.   Not the garden. The boathouse. *(Bobby kisses Ramon this time, passionately, and then disappears back into the lake. Ramon watches him disappear. After a while, he will lie back down and sleep. Buzz joins James in the shaded area.)*

JAMES.   No! I won't even say it. It's not possible. Do you think? Dare we dream?

BUZZ.   What?

JAMES.   This book says John F. Kennedy, Jr., is gay.

BUZZ.   That explains it. *(He has seen the rolling tray of refreshments.)* Is that for us? *(He goes to it.)*

JAMES.   That explains what?

BUZZ.   I've seen him in the Spike. It's a leather bar in Chelsea. He comes in with friends. Daryl Hannah, the Schlossbergs, Willy Smith.

JAMES.   I don't believe it.

BUZZ.   I'm the wrong person to ask. I think everyone is gay, and if they're not, they should be. *(He calls off to the raft:)* Ramon! Noon! Teatime! *(Ramon doesn't react.)* He doesn't hear me. He's going to burn to a crisp. Ramon! If that was my boyfriend, I would swim out there and drag him in by the hair.

JAMES.   If he were my boyfriend, he could do anything he wanted.

BUZZ.   I know what you mean. Maybe that's why I don't have a boyfriend. I'm too caring. *(They are both looking out across the lake to Ramon.)*

JAMES.   My brother has always had a good-looking man in his life.

BUZZ.   Thank you.

JAMES.   I beg your pardon?

BUZZ.   He didn't tell you? It was when he first came to this country. Short and sweet. Six months, tops.

JAMES.   I'm sorry. What happened?

BUZZ.   We were both very young. I was too needy. He wasn't needy enough.

JAMES.   I don't think John can love anyone.

BUZZ.   Now you tell me!

JAMES.   Perhaps one of us had better go out there and tell Ramon.

BUZZ.   I'll let you break it to him. I don't think I'm his type.

JAMES.   I don't think either of us is. *(They are both still staring out across the lake to Ramon on the raft.)* I enjoy looking, though. *(Buzz and James sigh.)*

BUZZ.   Is there a British equivalent for "machismo?"

JAMES.   No. None at all. Maybe Glenda Jackson.

BUZZ.   Do you have a boyfriend over there?

JAMES.   Not anymore. What about you?

BUZZ.   *(Shaking his head.)* When the going gets tough, weak boyfriends get going. Or something like that.

JAMES.   I can't honestly say I'm minding. Last acts are depressing and generally one long solo.

BUZZ.   They don't have to be. *(Buzz finally looks at James.)* How sick are you?

JAMES.   I think I'm in pretty good nick, but my reports read like something out of Nostradamus. *(He looks at Buzz.)* I should have died six months ago.

BUZZ.   Try eighteen. Do you have any lesions?

JAMES.   Only one, and I've had it for nearly a year.

BUZZ.   Where is it?

JAMES.   In a very inconvenient spot.

BUZZ.   They're all inconvenient. May I see it?

JAMES.   It's — All right. *(He pulls up his shirt and lets Buzz see the lesion.)* I have a lesbian friend in London who's the only other person who's ever asked to see it. I was quite astonished when she did. Touched, actually. Mortified, too, of course. But mainly touched. Somebody loves me, even if it's not the someone I've dreamed of. A little love from a woman who works in the box office at the Lyric Hammersmith is better than none. Are you through? *(Buzz kisses the lesion.)* Gwyneth didn't go that far. It doesn't disgust you?

BUZZ.   It's going to be me.

JAMES.   You don't know that.

BUZZ.   Yes, I do.

JAMES.   You learn to make friends with them. Hello, little lesion. Not people you like especially, but people you've made your peace with.

BUZZ.   You're very nice, you know.

JAMES.   Frankly, I don't see how I can afford not to be.

BUZZ.   No, I mean it.

JAMES.   So are you.

BUZZ.   I didn't mean to interrupt your reading.

JAMES.   It was getting too intense. They just outed George and Ira Gershwin.

BUZZ.   Wait till they get to Comden and Green. Would you like me to bring you a real drink down? I know where they hide the good liquor.

JAMES.   An ice-cold martini. Very dry. With a twist.

BUZZ.   Is that going to be good for you?

JAMES.   Of course not.

BUZZ.   Does this make me an enabler?

JAMES.   No, but it makes me your slave for life. I'll snitch a frock out of National Theatre storage for you. Something of Dame Edith Evans'.

BUZZ.   What's the matter?

JAMES.   I'm waiting for you to tell me she was gay.

BUZZ.   She wasn't, actually. One of the two British actresses who isn't. I think Deborah Kerr is the other one. But all the rest — galloping lezzies! *(He goes. James looks after him and does not resume reading for quite some time. Gregory's leg is being tended to by Arthur. Perry watches squeamishly. Bobby is with them.)*

ARTHUR.   How's that?

GREGORY.   Ow.

PERRY.   Jesus, Gregory! I never really looked at your body before. I mean, except when you're on stage in a costume

56

and lights and I'm in the fifth row.

GREGORY. Well, don't start now.

PERRY. It's amazing.

GREGORY. It's just old. Um. And very used.

PERRY. Your legs are like knots. And your feet. I can't even look at them. Doesn't everything hurt?

GREGORY. Yes. They have for years.

PERRY. Why do you to it?

GREGORY. I don't know. I just know I don't know what I'd do if I didn't.

ARTHUR. Why do you practice law?

PERRY. Law doesn't do that to me.

BOBBY. Gregory says a dancer's body is the scars of his dancing.

GREGORY. Bobby.

BOBBY. Isn't that what you say?

GREGORY. To you. Now it sounds pretentious.

ARTHUR. It's not pretentious, Greg.

BOBBY. The dances are gone, but his body's effort to do them isn't. Show them, Gregory.

GREGORY. Here's the Philip Glass.

ARTHUR. Look, Perry.

PERRY. I can't.

GREGORY. Here's the Bach-Schoenberg. Here's the Ravel. The Sam Barber. Here's the best one of all: the David Diamond. *(Buzz enters.)*

BUZZ. I can't leave you kids alone for a second! Bobby bwana, you be having a phone call in the Big House.

BOBBY. Thanks, Buzz. Show them *Webern Pieces*.

GREGORY. There are no. Um. *Webern Pieces* yet.

BOBBY. There will be.

PERRY. There better be. We've signed the contracts.

BUZZ. I can understand not having a phone down here, but what has he got against an intercom? *(Buzz and Bobby go.)*

PERRY. While Arthur tended Gregory and I gaped at his life's wounds (his body didn't look old; it looked exhausted, spent — like that barren soil of Africa that can't produce anymore), and while James waited with more anticipation than he

57

realized for Buzz to return, and while Ramon bronzed his already brozen body even bronzer, Bobby was learning via a very iffy connection with a not very forthcoming sub-attaché at the American consulate in Jaipur that his sister, two years his senior, was dead. Valerie, I think her name was. Just like that.

BOBBY.   What? I can't hear you. You'll have to speak up.

PERRY.   It was a freak accident.

BOBBY.   What?

PERRY.   Something to do with a faultily installed ride at a fun fair at a religious festival celebrating the god Shiva.

BOBBY.   How? *(Gregory will join Bobby and put his arms around him from behind while he talks on the phone.)*

PERRY.   A sort of swing you sat in that spun around a sort of maypole. *(Arthur joins him.)*

ARTHUR.   We never got the full story. *(He rests his head on Perry's shoulder. James stops reading. Buzz comes out of the kitchen, mixing bowl in hand. Ramon sits up on the raft.)*

BOBBY.   Thank you for calling. *(He lets the phone drop.)*

GREGORY.   Oh, honey, I'm so sorry.

PERRY.   No one knew whether to stay or go. There is nothing quite like the vulnerability of weekend guests.

BOBBY.   It's all so fucking fragile. So fucking arbitrary.

GREGORY.   I know, I know.

ARTHUR.   It's not what we want. It's what Bobby wants.

BOBBY.   I want you to stay.

RAMON.   We stayed.

BOBBY.   Let's go upstairs. *(Bobby and Gregory leave. There is a silence. From the house Bobby is heard howling his grief: a wild, uncontainable animal sound.)*

JAMES.   Poor lamb. I'm afraid those martinis have made me quite, quite maudlin. I'm all teary. *(John is heard playing the piano, off: the Pas des Cygnes from Swan Lake.)*

PERRY.   *Swan Lake.* My blood just ran cold. Gregory is serious about that goddamn benefit.

JAMES.   So many costumes, so little time.

PERRY.   *(Calling off.)* Give it a rest, will you, John? *(He gives up.)*

JAMES.   Gregory says you're a good sport and you'll do it

in the end.

PERRY.   Gregory is wrong.

ARTHUR.   I'm working on him, James.

PERRY.   And you're not getting up in any goddamn tutu and toe shoes either.

ARTHUR.   My lord and master here. Do you want to go for a swim?

PERRY.   I want to get some sun.

ARTHUR.   We can swim and sun.

PERRY.   You just want to visit your boyfriend on the raft.

ARTHUR.   You want to talk about giving something a rest?

(James buries himself in his book and begins to read aloud.)

JAMES.   "No one who had ever seen Catherine Morland in her infancy would have supposed her born to be a heroine."

(Buzz has entered with more refreshments. He is wearing an apron, heels, and little else.)

BUZZ.   They said the same thing about me.

PERRY.   Jesus Christ, Buzz.

BUZZ.   What?

PERRY.   You know goddamn well what.

BUZZ.   No. What? This? *(He flashes Perry.)*

PERRY.   Put some clothes on. Nobody wants to look at that.

BUZZ.   That? You are calling my body "that"?

PERRY.   You're not at a nudist colony. There are other people present.

BUZZ.   I thought I was among friends.

PERRY.   I'm sure James here is just as uncomfortable as we are, only he's just too polite to say so.

JAMES.   James here is still reeling from the news about the Kennedy boy. You could all be starkers and I wouldn't bat an eyebrow.

PERRY.   Tell him, Arthur.

ARTHUR.   It's not bothering me.

BUZZ.   Thank you, Arthur. I'm glad Isadora Duncan and Sally Kirkland did not live entirely in vain.

PERRY.   Please, Buzz.

BUZZ.   No. Close your eyes. Take a walk. Drop dead.

PERRY.   What brought this on?

BUZZ. Nothing brought it on. Some people do things spontaneously. It's a beautiful day. The sun feels good. I may not be around next summer. Okay? This is what I look like, Perry. Sorry it's not better. It's the best I can do. Love me, love my love handles.

ARTHUR. That's what I keep telling him!

PERRY. None of us may be around next summer. *(Arthur starts undressing.)* What do you think you're doing?

ARTHUR. Come on, I'll race you out to the raft.

PERRY. Go to hell.

ARTHUR. I can't believe you actually lived through the sixties, Perry. We only read about them in Kansas, and I'm less uptight than you.

PERRY. You know, I could walk around like that, too, if I wanted to.

BUZZ. Who's stopping you?

PERRY. I just don't want to.

BUZZ. I think she's got it. By George, she's got it! *(Buzz and Arthur do a little celebratory twirl before he braves the lake waters.)*

PERRY. I give up. I hope your dick gets a sunburn.

ARTHUR. Yadda, yadda, yadda.

BUZZ. That's the spirit. The world loves a good sport. *(Arthur goes into the lake and starts to swim out to the float.)*

PERRY. Both your dicks!

BUZZ. I forgot my sunblock!

PERRY. Would you bring mine? It's on our dresser. The lip balm should be right with it.

BUZZ. I thought you were mad at me. I see! Get me waiting on you hand and foot and all is forgiven.

PERRY. Oh, and the Walkman. There's a Bob Dylan tape with it.

BUZZ. Bob Dylan? You sure you don't want Rosa Ponselle? Get a life, Perry. They've invented penicillin. You can actually pick up a phone and talk to someone in New Jersey now.

PERRY. I still like Bob Dylan — and don't tell me he's gay.

BUZZ. For his sake, I hope he's not. Would you date him?

PERRY. That's cruel.

BUZZ. I know. So's dating. *(He goes. Arthur has reached the raft. He is winded from the swim.)*

RAMON.   I'll race you back in!

ARTHUR.   What? No. I just got here.

RAMON.   Aw, c'mon.

ARTHUR.   No, I said. Give me a hand. *(Ramon helps Arthur onto the raft.)*

RAMON.   I'll let you catch your breath. Then we'll race.

ARTHUR.   My breath is fine. We're not racing. *(He flops on the raft. Ramon stays in a sitting up position.)*

RAMON.   I hate the country. I fucking hate it. There's no cabs to get you fucking out of it. I like mass transportation. I like the fucking pavement under my feet. I like places that sell food that stay open all night. I fucking hate it.

PERRY.   Should I be trusting my lover skinny-dipping with a horny Puerto Rican modern dancer?

JAMES.   It depends on what makes you suspicious. Horny, Puerto Rican, modern, or dancer?

PERRY.   All of them.

JAMES.   How long have you two been together?

PERRY.   Fourteen years. We're role models. It's very stressful.

JAMES.   Two or three years was the most I ever managed. Mutual lack of attention span. *(Buzz returns.)*

BUZZ.   Here's your desperate attempt to stay young, Mr. Sellars. *Blood on the Tracks.* Wasn't this originally released on 78s?

PERRY.   Bob Dylan will go down in history as one of the great American songwriters. *(He puts on the headset and lies back.)*

BUZZ.   He's no Lerner and Loewe! *(He is getting ready to settle down, too.)* Wake me if I doze off. I have a VCR alert for AMC. *Damn Yankees* at one-thirty. Gwen Verdon is hosting. Poor James, you don't have a clue what I'm talking about.

JAMES.   I seldom know what any American is talking about. *(Reading:)* "No one who had ever seen Catherine Morland in her infancy would have supposed her born to be a heroine."

BUZZ.   I love being read to. I feel five years old. *(Perry sings along with his Dylan tape. James reads to Buzz. John is playing the*

piano. Ramon smacks Arthur on his bare ass.)
ARTHUR.   Ow!
RAMON.   You had a fly on you. You know, you got a nice ass for someone your age.
ARTHUR.   Thank you.
RAMON.   You both do.
ARTHUR.   Thank you.
RAMON.   I really hate it. *(Gregory and Bobby are in their room.)*
GREGORY.   When is the body—?
BOBBY.   Not until Tuesday.
GREGORY.   So long?
BOBBY.   Red tape. She always said there was nothing worse than Indian red tape. We're meeting it in Dallas. I'll fly down Monday.
GREGORY.   I think we should both fly down tonight.
BOBBY.   No. You stay here and work. I want you to finish the piece. It's more important.
GREGORY.   It's all important. Why don't you want to go down there tonight?
BOBBY.   We've got a houseful.
GREGORY.   I'll manage.
BOBBY.   We'll see. Do you know what this music is?
GREGORY.   No. But it's Russian. It's definitely Russian. There are times I wish you could see me.
BOBBY.   I see you, Gregory.
GREGORY.   See me looking at you. The love there. I'm not —
BOBBY.   I know.
GREGORY.   It only happens when I'm alone with you. It's like a little present. I know this is a terrible thing to say right now, but I am so happy, Bobby. Thank you, God, for him.
BOBBY.   You know how we tell each other everything, even when it's hard?
GREGORY.   Yes.
BOBBY.   I'd like to make this one of those times.
GREGORY.   All right.
BOBBY.   Memorial Day weekend.
GREGORY.   Yes.
BOBBY.   Something happened.

GREGORY. Why do I have a feeling I don't want to hear this?

BOBBY. Ramon and I.

GREGORY. Don't, Bobby. Don't.

BOBBY. We made love. I didn't want it to happen, but it did.

GREGORY. Is there more?

BOBBY. No. I'm sorry.

GREGORY. So am I.

BOBBY. This was better than not telling you, Gregory. *(Gregory is starting to have difficulty speaking again.)*

GREGORY. It's Scriabin. Um. The music, it's. Um. It's definitely Scriabin.

BOBBY. Talk to me, Gregory.

GREGORY. Have you. Did you. Do you. Want to. Again?

BOBBY. No, I'm with you.

GREGORY. You're. Um. Very lucky you. Um. Can't. Um. See right now, Robert. Go to Texas tonight. I don't want you in our house.

BOBBY. Where are you going?

GREGORY. Down to the lake. Don't. Um. Come. Um. With me. Um. It's back. That was brief. *(He goes. Bobby comes forward to us.)*

BOBBY. Do you believe in God? Don't worry, I'm not going to fall off this time! Do you? I think we all believe in God in our way. Or want to. Or need to. Only so many of us are afraid to. Unconditional love is pretty terrifying. We don't think we deserve it. It's human nature to run. But He always finds us. He never gives up. I used to think that's what other people were for. Lovers, friends, family. I had it all wrong. Other people are as imperfect and as frightened as we are. We love, but not unconditionally. Only God is unconditional love, and we don't even have to love Him back. He's very big about it. I have a lot of reservations about God. What intelligent, caring person doesn't lately? But the way I see it, He doesn't have any reservations about me. It's very one-sided. It's unconditional. Besides, He's God. I'm not. *(He goes. Arthur stirs on the raft.)*

63

ARTHUR. Sun like this makes you want to never move again. I feel nailed to this raft. Crucified on it.

RAMON. Sun like this makes me horny.

ARTHUR. Well ...

RAMON. I bet I can hold my breath underwater longer than you.

ARTHUR. I bet you can, too.

RAMON. Come on, you want to see?

ARTHUR. No! If you re so bored ...

RAMON. Come on!

ARTHUR. I don't want to. Play with someone else.

RAMON. Come on! *Venga*, baby, *venga!*

ARTHUR. I'm resting. It's a national holiday.

RAMON. Come on! You know you want to! Don't be an old fart! Who knows? We get down there together, who knows what might happen? Yeah? *(He jumps off the raft and goes under the water.)*

ARTHUR. Damn it. You got me all — Shit. I was nice and dry. I'm not going in there. I don't care how long you stay under. You can drown, Ramon. I hope you can hear me down there. You're not getting me in. All right, Ramon. That's enough. Come on. Stop. *(Gregory appears at the side of the raft. He hangs there.)*

PERRY. I remember when Gregory bought this place. I was dead against it. "It's in the middle of nowhere. What are you going to do for fun?" Now it seems like bliss. No one for miles and miles. We could be the last eight people on earth.

BUZZ. That's a frightening thought.

JAMES. Not if you're with the right eight people. Who's that out there on the raft?

BUZZ. It looks like Gregory.

PERRY. Where's Arthur? He was out there.

BUZZ. You're looking good, Gregory!

PERRY. Arthur? Arthur? He was with Ramon.

BUZZ. We'd better put a stop to that. Arthur! Your mother wants you. Arthur! The *MacNeil/Lehrer Report* is on. Arthur! *(To Perry and James:)* Help me. One, two, three.

BUZZ, PERRY, and JAMES. Arthur!! *(Buzz starts coughing. He can't stop.)*

JAMES.   Are you all right?

BUZZ.   Ooooo!

JAMES.   Here.

BUZZ.   Thank you.

JAMES.   Just get your breath. Lean on me. There you go.

BUZZ.   Look at Gregory out there. He's lucky. He is so lucky.

JAMES.   So are we.

BUZZ.   Not like that. Not like that. *(In the silence, we will begin to notice the throbbing, humming sounds of summer's high noon. The figure of Gregory on the raft glows, shimmers, irradiates in the bright light. Nothing moves.)*

JAMES.   Listen. What's that sound?

PERRY.   Nature.

JAMES.   It's fearful.

PERRY.   It's life.

BUZZ.   It's so loud.

PERRY.   Because we're listening to it. Ssshh.

BUZZ.   I never —

JAMES.   Ssshh.

PERRY.   Arthur and I were in Alaska once. We flew out to a glacier. When the pilot cut the engine, it was so quiet you could hear the universe throbbing. I didn't know it did that. It was thrilling. *(Tableau. The three men do not move. James has his arm around Buzz. Gregory is sitting on the raft with his knees pulled up to his chin. He is crying. There is a distant but ominous roll of thunder.)* Five minutes later, it was raining buckets. Thunder, lightning, wind. Everybody scattered. James, take the hammock in. Gregory! Come in! Lightning!

BUZZ.   Auntie Em! Auntie Em!

PERRY.   Buzz, run the flag down. Where is my Arthur? Arthur!! *(Arthur appears, fully dressed and dry. He will join Perry.)*

ARTHUR.   Your Arthur was gasping for breath on the other side of the lake. *(Ramon appears; he is not dressed and he is still wet. He is laughing and playful.)*

RAMON.   I knew I'd get you in!

ARTHUR.   You scared me. I thought something had happened to you.

RAMON.   I wanted to stay down there forever. I wished I was a fish.

ARTHUR.   He was sitting on the bottom of the lake. When I swam up to him he pulled me towards him and kissed me on the mouth.

RAMON.   I was goofing.

ARTHUR.   Then he swam away.

PERRY.   In all the excitement, the tragedy of Bobby's sister was quite forgotten. Where were you?

ARTHUR.   Nowhere. I was swimming. Their door is still closed. You were right, Perry, we should have left.

PERRY.   Don't do that.

ARTHUR.   Do what?

PERRY.   Disappear.

RAMON.   *(Holding a magazine.)* Okay, here he is, I found him. Gather round, gentlemen.

BUZZ.   It was after lunch and Ramon was having a hard time convincing us of an adventure he claimed to have had on the island of Mykonos.

RAMON.   That's him. I swear on my mother's life.

BUZZ.   And I had sex with the ghost of Troy Donahue.

PERRY.   First you said he was the model for Calvin Klein's Obsession. Now he's the model for —

RAMON.   I can't keep all those names straight, but I don't forget a face and body like that.

BUZZ.   You all know the picture.

ARTHUR.   And you found this person in the same position sleeping adrift in a fishing boat?

RAMON.   Yes. You ever been to Greece? There are a lot of fishing boats. Why won't you believe he was in one of them?

PERRY.   And you made love to him?

RAMON.   Not in the fishing boat. It started raining. We went ashore. We found sort of a cave.

JAMES.   This is very Dido and Aeneas. I'm calling Barbara Cartland. *(He goes.)*

RAMON.   Why would I make up a story like that? It's too incredible.

PERRY. You're right, it is.

RAMON. Fuck you, all of you. I don't care. But the next time you see his picture or you're tossing in your beds thinking about him, just remember: somebody had him and it wasn't you. I know how that must burn your asses.

BUZZ. Go to your room! *(He goes. The others stay with the magazine.)*

ARTHUR. Do you think he's telling the truth?

BUZZ. No, do you?

PERRY. The thought of Ramon and his possible encounter with the Obsession Man hung over the house like a shroud. We all wanted him and never would —

BUZZ. I bet he's got a rotten personality.

PERRY. Anyway. There is nothing like the steady drumming of a summer rain on wooden shingles to turn even this pedantic mind into a devil's workshop. I've got an idea. *(He whispers to Arthur and Buzz, who surround him. Ramon and John are seen in their room.)*

RAMON. I don't know people like you and your friends. I don't know what you're talking about half the time. Who the fuck are Dido and Aeneas? We used to beat up people like you where I grew up.

JOHN. Come here.

RAMON. Do you believe me?

JOHN. Do you want me to believe you?

RAMON. Maybe.

JOHN. So come here. *(Ramon will take his time coming over to where John is.)*

PERRY. Unfortunately, John and Ramon were not alone. Buzz and I had hidden in their closet. Our plan was to leap out at the moment of maximum inopportunity and embarrassment and then regale the rest of the household with what we'd seen and heard.

BUZZ. It'll serve John right.

PERRY. What does that mean?

BUZZ. Never mind. Squeeze!

RAMON. What? *(John kisses Ramon.)*

PERRY. It was a terrible idea. Arthur would have no part

of it.

ARTHUR. Happy anniversary to you, too, Perry! *(He goes.)*

PERRY. Is today the — I'm sorry, Arthur. Oh, shit.

JOHN. What's the matter?

RAMON. I thought I heard something.

PERRY. That was our last chance. We should have taken it.

JOHN. Sit down.

RAMON. You want to? Now?

JOHN. Sit.

RAMON. I'm a little sunburned.

JOHN. Sit.

RAMON. Aren't you going to lock the door?

JOHN. It's locked. Sit. *(Ramon sits in a straight-back chair.)* Put your hands behind your back. Feet apart. Head down. Ready for interrogation. My beautiful bound prisoner. Look at me. You look so beautiful like that. I think I could come without even touching you.

BUZZ. Oh!

RAMON. I think I could, too. Let me go.

JOHN. No.

RAMON. Please. The rope. It's too tight. My wrists, the circulation.

JOHN. Go on, struggle.

RAMON. I can't get loose.

JOHN. Look at me. Don't take your eyes from mine. Who do you see?

RAMON. No one. You! Let me touch you.

JOHN. Not yet. Who do you see? Who do you wish I were?

RAMON. No, I won't tell you.

JOHN. Yes, you will. Who? Look at me. Look at me! Who? Who do you wish I were?

RAMON. Kiss me. Gag me with your mouth. *(John kisses him.)*

PERRY. We knew what they were doing. We didn't have to see.

BUZZ. I was singing "99 Bottles of Beer on the Wall" silently to myself. It's a very hard song to sing silently to yourself.

RAMON. Who do you see? Who do you want in this chair?

68

JOHN. I don't know.

RAMON. Yes, you do. Everybody does. Who do you see? Who do you want here like this? Tell me, it's okay, John.

JOHN. I can't.

RAMON. Who? Come on, baby, who?

JOHN. Don't make me.

RAMON. I can't make you do anything. I'm your fucking prisoner, man. You got me tied up here. Gagged. Mmmm. Mmmm.

JOHN. His name was Padraic. The Irish spelling.

RAMON. Fuck the spelling!

JOHN. Padraic Boyle. He was seventeen years old. I was nineteen.

RAMON. I hear you. Seventeen and nineteen!

JOHN. He will always be seventeen years old and I will always be nineteen. Neither of us grows old in this story.

RAMON. What did he look like, this hot fucking stud Irishman?

JOHN. He was a fierce-looking ginger Irishman with big powerful shoulders and arms with muscles with big veins in them. You could see them blue through the white skin of his biceps. Always in hip boots and a vest.

RAMON. A vest? He was wearing a fucking vest?

JOHN. I'm sorry — undershirts, you call them.

RAMON. That's more like it. Fucking Fruit of the Looms, fucking BVDs, fucking Calvins.

JOHN. He worked for us. So did his father. We owned a fleet of coaches. Padraic and his father washed them. But that didn't matter. We were friends. He liked me. I know he liked me.

RAMON. Cut to the chase.

JOHN. Cut to what chase? There wasn't any chase.

RAMON. It's a movie expression. Get to the good part.

JOHN. It's all good part.

RAMON. Get to the sex. One night...!

JOHN. One day we started wrestling. It was summer. He was washing a coach (that's a bus), and —

RAMON. I know what a coach is. I've been to London.

JOHN.   And Padraic squirted me with a hose and I got him with a bucket of water and then we started fooling around, and one thing led to another and we started wrestling, we were in the garage now, and suddenly Padraic put his hand down there and he could feel I was hard and he said, "What is this? What the bloody hell is this, mate?"

RAMON.   What did you do?

JOHN.   I put my hand on him down there and he was hard and I said, "And what the bloody hell is that, mate?" and we both laughed, but we didn't move.

PERRY.   Even from the closet, we were beginning to share Ramon's impatience.

PERRY and BUZZ.   Cut to the fucking chase!

JOHN.   He stopped laughing. "Do you know what we're doing?" I had no idea, so I nodded yes. He took off my belt and wrapped it around my wrists. He raised my arms over my head and hung them to a hook along the wall. I probably could have freed myself. I didn't try. He took out a handkerchief and gagged me with it. Then, and this frightened me, he ripped open my shirt. Then he unfastened my trousers and let them drop to my ankles. Then he undressed himself and took a chair, very like this one, and sat in it, maybe five feet away from me. He had some rope. He wrapped it around his wrists like he was tied to the chair. He'd gagged himself, too, with his own knickers. He looked right at me. He didn't move. Not even the slightest undulation of his hips, and then he came and all he'd let out was this one, soft "oh." After a while, he opened his eyes, asked me how I was doing and cleaned himself up. Then he stood up and kissed me lightly on the lips. No man had ever kissed me on the lips before. I wanted to kiss him back, but I didn't dare. He moved to whisper something in my ear. My heart stopped beating. He was going to tell me he loved me! Instead, he said, "I've doused this place with petrol. I'm lighting a match. You have three minutes to get out alive. Good luck, 007." And then he laughed and walked out whistling. He never wanted to play again. The last time I saw him he was overweight, the father of four and still washing our coaches. But that's who I still see there. Every time. And that's why we hate the bloody Irish!

PERRY.   Clearly the mood was broken. I felt a certain relief.

(Gregory appears outside their door.)

GREGORY.   Knock, knock!

JOHN.   Yes?

GREGORY.   Can I. Um. Get in there a sec?

JOHN.   Sure.

RAMON.   *(Playfully.)* Maybe Greg can rescue me. *(He puts his arms behind him, struggles again.)* Mmmmm. Mmmmm, Help.

JOHN.   Stop that. *(Gregory comes into the room.)*

GREGORY.   Sorry. I need to. Um. Get a suitcase. Um. For Bobby.

RAMON.   *(Playfully.)* Mmmmmm! Mmmmmm!

JOHN.   Ignore him. *(Gregory opens the closet and sees Perry and Buzz.)*

PERRY.   *(To Gregory.)* Ssshh. Please. I'll explain.

JOHN.   Was it in there?

GREGORY.   No. Wrong closet.

RAMON.   Help! Mmmmm. *(Gregory goes. Buzz manages to exit with him without being seen by John or Ramon.)* It sounds like Bobby's leaving. I want to say goodbye. Do you mind if we don't —

JOHN.   Suit yourself.

RAMON.   I'm not Padraic.

JOHN.   And I'm not Bobby. *C'est la vie.*

RAMON.   I don't know what you're talking about. *(He goes.)*

JOHN.   Wait up. I'll go with you.

PERRY.   I suppose the next few moments could be called out of the closet and into the fire. John had forgotten his wallet. People like John don't feel fully dressed unless they're carrying their wallets, even on Fourth of July weekends on forty-plus acres.

JOHN.   You son of a bitch.

PERRY.   I'm sorry.

JOHN.   You miserable son of a bitch.

PERRY.   It was a joke. It was supposed to be funny.

JOHN.   You scum. You lump. You piece of shit. How dare you?

PERRY. I wasn't thinking. I'm sorry, John. I have never been sorrier about anything in my entire life.

JOHN. How fucking dare you?

PERRY. I will get down on my knees to you to ask your forgiveness.

JOHN. What did you hear?

PERRY. Nothing.

JOHN. What did you hear?

PERRY. I won't tell anyone. Not even Arthur. I swear on my mother's life, I won't. *(John spits in Perry's face.)*

JOHN. I hope you get what my brother has. I hope you die from it. When I read or hear that you have, then, then, Perry, will I forgive you. *(He goes.)*

PERRY. I don't know which was worse. His words or his saliva. Right now I can't think of anything more annihilating than being spat upon. I could feel his hate running down my face. So much for the unsafe exchange of body fluids. *(Arthur is trimming the hair in Perry's ears.)*

ARTHUR. I'm glad you're getting your sense of humor back. I'd like to flatten that limey motherfucker. I'm tired of "limey." Aren't there any other hateful words for those cocksucking, ass-licking, motherfucking, shit-eating descendants of Shakespeare, Shelley, and Keats?

PERRY. Come on, honey. Let's drop it.

ARTHUR. I don't go around hitting people or using words like "motherfucker," but that's how mad I am.

PERRY. Let it go. I love my bracelet. Thank you.

ARTHUR. Happy anniversary.

PERRY. I'm sorry I forgot. What do you want?

ARTHUR. Towels.

PERRY. Towels? That's not very romantic.

ARTHUR. The last time your mother stayed with us I could see she thought the towels were my responsibility. It's one thing for her son to be gay just so long as he's not the one who's doing the cooking. Towels and a Mixmaster!

PERRY. Who wound you up?

ARTHUR. That asshole did. Don't get me started again. He's just lucky I'm a big queen.

PERRY.   Don't forget the left ear.

ARTHUR.   And you're really lucky I'm a big queen.

PERRY.   One thing you're not, Arthur, and never will be is a big queen.

ARTHUR.   I know. I'm butch. One of the lucky ones. I can catch a ball. I genuinely like both my parents. I hate opera. I don't know why I bother being gay.

PERRY.   I was so sure you weren't that first time I saw you. I came this close to not saying hello. *(Perry suddenly kisses one of Arthur's hands.)*

ARTHUR.   Where did that come from?

PERRY.   Are we okay?

ARTHUR.   We're fine. Don't rock de boat. It don't need no rocking. Fourteen years! Make you feel old?

PERRY.   No, lucky.

ARTHUR.   My first time in New York. You had your own apartment in "Green-wich Village." Exposed brick. I was so impressed.

PERRY.   It's pronounced Greenwich. You're lucky you were so cute.

ARTHUR.   The Mark Spitz poster right out where anyone could see it. *(Buzz crosses the room.)*

BUZZ.   He's gay, you know.

ARTHUR.   He is?

BUZZ.   They're all gay. The entire Olympics.

PERRY.   This is my roommate, Buzz. Buzz, this is — I'm sorry —

ARTHUR.   Arthur.

PERRY.   Oh come on, I didn't —

ARTHUR.   You did.

PERRY.   Why are we whispering?

BUZZ.   I've got someone in my room. He's a Brit. I'm getting him tea. *(Now John crosses the room.)*

JOHN.   Don't mind me, ducks. Just nipping through. Is that the loo? *(He goes.)*

BUZZ.   Don't say anything, Perry. I think he's cute. He's written a musical. I think I'm in love.

PERRY.   Take it easy this time, will you?

73

BUZZ.   Perry likes it rough, Arthur — really, really rough.
(He goes.)
ARTHUR.   He was right — you did.
PERRY.   Look who's talking! Do you want me to do your
ears now?
ARTHUR.   That was John? I'd completely forgotten. He and
Buzz met the same night we did. We lasted, they didn't.
PERRY.   I thought you were the most wonderful looking man
I'd ever seen.
ARTHUR.   Did you? Did you really think that?
PERRY.   Unh-hunh.
ARTHUR.   Ow!
PERRY.   Sorry. When was the last time I did this?
ARTHUR.   Don't make a face.
PERRY.   I'm not making a face.
ARTHUR.   I can hear it in your voice.
PERRY.   I wouldn't do this for anyone but you.
ARTHUR.   You know, if you really think about it, this is what
it all comes down to.
PERRY.   What? Trimming the hair in your boyfriend's ears?
Oh God, I hope not. *(Buzz and James appear. They are ready for
a tutu fitting. James motions Arthur and Perry to come close.)*
ARTHUR.   That and helping your best friends out by put-
ting on a tutu for five minutes in front of three thousand
people in Carnegie Hall. *(Buzz and James have put a tape mea-
sure around Perry's waist. Buzz drapes him in tulle.)*
PERRY.   You're wasting your time, Buzz, I'm not going to
do it. *(Buzz writes down the measurements.)*
BUZZ.   She's a classic *Giselle* size, I should have guessed.
Thirty-six! Whose measurements are these?
JAMES.   Yours, luv.
ARTHUR.   Is that good or bad?
JAMES.   For a tutu it's a little big. For a gay man it's a di-
saster.
BUZZ.   I'm not thirty-six! What metric system are you on?
Let me see that. What are you laughing at? You're next. *(Buzz
and James pursue Arthur off.)*
PERRY.   Anyway. The heavens cleared. The sunset was spec-

tacular. The next day would be glorious. We would have a fabulous Fifth of July, sodden fireworks and strained relationships notwithstanding. Only the evening lay ahead. *(The sound of crickets. Bobby is waiting in the yard with his suitcase. It is night. Ramon appears.)*

RAMON. Hi.

BOBBY. Hi. Betty's Taxi is living up to their reputation. "We're on our way, Mr. Brahms." Five minutes, she promised, and that was twenty minutes ago.

RAMON. I have a sister, too. I love her very much. I'm sorry.

BOBBY. Thank you, Ramon.

RAMON. Where's your cowboy boots? They told me home for you was Texas. I thought you'd be in boots and a Stetson.

BOBBY. Home for me is right here. My folks are in Texas. Paris, Texas.

RAMON. Aw, c'mon. There's no such place.

BOBBY. French is my second language.

RAMON. You're kidding.

BOBBY. I'm kidding. The settlers had delusions of grandeur. *(Ramon takes his hand.)* Don't.

RAMON. I'm sorry. *(He lets go of Bobby's hand.)*

BOBBY. A part of me is, too. I can't.

RAMON. Does Gregory—?

BOBBY. No.

RAMON. That night by the refrigerator...?

BOBBY. Any of it. *(Gregory appears outside the house.)*

GREGORY. You're still here?

BOBBY. They're on their way.

RAMON. Safe trip, amigo. I'm really sorry. *(He goes back into the house.)*

GREGORY. I would have driven you. Um. In. Um.

BOBBY. We've got guests.

GREGORY. We both need time to think.

BOBBY. I don't. I'm sorry. I love you.

GREGORY. *(He is angry.)* Are any of you. Um. Gardeners? I'm especially. Um. Proud of what I've done here. Um. It's a. Um. Seasonal garden. Always something blooming. Um. Just as another dies. That's a. Um. Bobby knows the names of everything. *Dianthus barbatus.* That's the Latin name. Um. I can't think of the. Um. Common one.

BOBBY.   Sweet William. It's Sweet William. And this one is rue. Bitter. Very bitter. Buzz says I would make a great Ophelia if I wouldn't fall off the stage.

GREGORY.   He shouldn't. Um. Say things like that. Um. To you. *(He is crying.)*

BOBBY.   And this is. Wait. Don't tell me.

GREGORY.   It's a rose.

BOBBY.   I know it's a rose. Connecticut Pride Morning Rose.

GREGORY.   I'll never understand it. The will to know the names of things you'll never see.

BOBBY.   It's one way of feeling closer to you. *(Gregory embraces Bobby, but they don't kiss.)*

GREGORY.   Hurry back to me. *(He goes back into the house. Bobby will stay in the yard until his cab comes. The other men have gathered in the living room. The TV is on.)*

BUZZ.   It's not my turn to clear up. I'm waiting for the musical remake of *Lost Horizon*. I never miss a chance to watch Liv Ullmann sing and dance.

JAMES.   May I join you? *(He sits next to Buzz.)*

ARTHUR.   What's this?

PERRY.   Open it.

ARTHUR.   You didn't forget. You had me fooled.

JAMES.   What are we watching?

BUZZ.   The *Dinah Shore Classic.* Dykes playing golf in the desert.

PERRY.   Do you like it?

ARTHUR.   I love it. Look, guys. A solar-power calculator.

PERRY.   For your work. Arthur's an accountant.

RAMON.   Very nice.

BUZZ.   Switching channels! *(We hear Bobby's cab tooting off. Bobby takes up his suitcase and goes to it. Gregory watches him through the window.)* Oh, look, the President's on MTV! He's made a video.

PERRY.   Only in America!

BUZZ.   He's gay, you know.

PERRY.   Dream on, Buzz.

BUZZ.   Why not? We could have a gay president.

PERRY.   It'll never happen.

BUZZ.   We're going to have a gay president in this country, you'll see.

PERRY.   It's the Fourth of July, Buzz, no gay rights stuff, please. *(Ramon gives the appointed "signal.")*

RAMON.   Are we having dessert or what?

BUZZ.   No dessert. You're too fat. We're all too fat.

RAMON.   My friend in the fishing boat didn't think I was too fat.

BUZZ.   Stay out of that kitchen. We're all on diets. *(Buzz, James, and Ramon go into the kitchen.)*

ARTHUR.   Go to CNN.

PERRY.   Not a moment too soon. I'd like to know what's going on in the world. *(Gregory is apart from the others.)*

ARTHUR.   Cheer up, Gregory. He's coming back.

GREGORY.   Thanks, Arthur.

ARTHUR.   That looks like Gore.

PERRY.   It's a gay demonstration in Seattle. The Vice-President is out there speaking up for endangered species. I don't think we were included. Jesus! Did you see that? He whacked that guy with his nightstick right against his head. Motherfucker!

GREGORY.   What's happening? *(He joins them in front of the TV set.)*

PERRY.   Why do they have to hit them like that? Jesus! *(They watch in silence. Appalling sounds of violence are coming from the television.)*

ARTHUR.   I can't watch this.

GREGORY.   Um. Um. Um.

ARTHUR.   It's okay, Greg, it's okay. Turn that off, will you?

PERRY.   What is wrong with this country? They hate us. They fucking hate us. They've always hated us. It never ends, the fucking hatred. *(The lights in the room go off. Buzz, James, and Ramon bring in a cake with blazing candles.)*

BUZZ, JAMES, RAMON, and GREGORY.   *(Singing.)*

Happy anniversary to you,

Happy anniversary to you,
Happy anniversary, Arthur and Perry,
Happy anniversary to you.
Make a wish. Speech, speech.

PERRY.   I'm married to the best man in the world, even if
he doesn't put the toothpaste cap back on and squeezes the
tube in the middle. I wish him long life, much love, and as
much happiness as he's brought me.

ARTHUR.   Ditto.

PERRY.   Ditto? That's it? Ditto? *(They begin a slow dance together.)*

JAMES.   That's nice.

BUZZ.   You don't have to go all Goody Two Shoes on us.

ARTHUR.   Everybody dance. All lovers dance.

BUZZ.   What about us single girls? *(To James:)* You know
you're dying to ask me. *(He starts dancing with James. There are
two couples dancing now.)*

PERRY.   So what was your wish? *(Arthur whispers something in
his ear.)* No fucking way, José. He still thinks you're going to
get me into one of those fucking tutus. *(Perry now leads Arthur.
They dance very well together. Buzz and James are dancing closer and
closer in a smaller and smaller space. Pretty soon they're just standing, holding on to each other, their arms around each other. Gregory
sits apart. Ramon watches them all.)* Arthur, look.

ARTHUR.   What?

PERRY.   Answered prayers. *(The two couples dance. Ramon and
Gregory sit staring at each other. The lights fade swiftly. The music
continues until the house lights are up.)*

ACT THREE

Dawn. Gregory is alone in his studio. Perry is sleeping with Arthur. James and Buzz are walking by the lake. Ramon and Bobby are both awake.

PERRY.   Gregory was stuck. He had been since the beginning of summer. And here it was Labor Day weekend. You'd think he'd move on, but Gregory is stubborn. I don't know if I admire that. *(Ramon steals from his bed.)*
RAMON.   Bobby?
PERRY.   So was Ramon.
RAMON.   Bobby?
PERRY.   I don't know if I admire that, either.
ARTHUR.   You're taking all the covers.
RAMON.   Bobby, it's me.
PERRY.   You hear that? They are up to something.
ARTHUR.   Mind your own business.
RAMON.   He's out in the studio. I can see the lights. I won't do anything. I just want to.... Fuck it. I'll be downstairs making coffee. *(He goes.)*
PERRY.   I wonder if Gregory had counted on Ramon showing up with John. I remembered the time Arthur had been unfaithful and how badly I'd handled it. I don't know what to say anymore and I certainly don't know what to do. "Don't ask, don't tell." No, that's something else. I prayed for good weather, took a Unisom, and wrapped myself around my Arthur. *(He rolls over and sleeps with Arthur.)*
ARTHUR.   No funny stuff. Go back to sleep. *(Gregory puts on the* Webern Opus 27 *and plays the same passage over and over.)*
BOBBY.   Gregory's not stubborn. He's scared. He's started telling people the new piece is nearly done when the truth is there's nothing there. I want to tell him to just stay in the moment, not to think in finished dances. That it doesn't have to be about everything. Just to let it come from here. But when I do he says, "What do you know about it? You're blind.

79

You betrayed me." It hasn't been easy since I got back from Texas.

GREGORY.   Shit.

BOBBY.   I wish it were just the two of us this weekend. *(John appears with Gregory's journal.)*

JOHN.   The lawns were brown now, the gardens wilted. The autumnal chill in the air was telling us this would be our last weekend. Soon it would be "back to school." Manderley had changed once again, but I hadn't. Still hung up on Ramon and our rituals. Still reading what other eyes were never meant to see. *(Reading from the journal.)* "James Jeckyll has decided to stay in this country. Buzz says he will get much better care here. He will also get Buzz. They are in love. I'm glad it happened here. Who could not love James? We have all taken him to our hearts. It will be a sad day when the light goes out."

GREGORY.   Shit, shit, shit, shit, shit!!! *(He stops dancing in a rage of utter frustration. He picks up a chair and smashes it again and again until it is in pieces. He falls to his knees and begins to cry.)*

PERRY.   I can't sleep. You didn't hear that?

ARTHUR.   Will you leave them alone?

PERRY.   Who?

ARTHUR.   Other people. All of them. You're as bad as John. And stop taking all the covers.

PERRY.   I'm not as bad as John. No one is as bad as John. I smell coffee. Do you smell coffee?

ARTHUR.   That's it! I want a divorce.

PERRY.   Are you awake now?

ARTHUR.   Thanks to you.

PERRY.   I'll bring you up some. How do you want it?

ARTHUR.   Black with eleven sugars. How do I want it?

PERRY.   You take it with milk, with Equal.

ARTHUR.   Why is he torturing me? *(Perry rolls out of bed.)*

PERRY.   It looks like rain. *(He goes.)*

JAMES.   I'm so cold, I'm so cold.

BUZZ.   I'm right here.

JAMES.   Two hours ago I was drenched in sweat.

BUZZ. Tonight'll be my turn.

JAMES. We're a fine pair.

BUZZ. We're loverly. I wouldn't have it any other way.

JAMES. I left England for this?

BUZZ. How are you feeling?

JAMES. Not sexy.

BUZZ. How are you feeling, really?

JAMES. "We defy augury."

BUZZ. What does that mean?

JAMES. I don't know. It's from a Shakespearean play we did at the National. The actor who played it always tossed his head and put his hand on his hip when he said it. I think he was being brave in the face of adversity.

BUZZ. Would this have been Lady Derek Jacobi or Dame Ian McKellen?

JAMES. I believe I have the floor! So, whenever I don't like what's coming down, I toss my head, put my hand on my hip, and say "We defy augury."

BUZZ. Shakespeare was gay, you know.

JAMES. You're going too far now.

BUZZ. Do you think a straight man would write a line like "We defy augury"? Get real, James. My three-year-old gay niece knows Shakespeare was gay. So was Anne Hathaway. So was her cottage. So was Julius Caesar. So was Romeo and Juliet. So was Hamlet. So was King Lear. Every character Shakespeare wrote was gay. Except for Titus Andronicus. Titus was straight. Go figure.

JAMES. People are awake.

BUZZ. I'll get us some coffee. *(He goes to the upstairs bathroom, where Perry is standing with his back to us. Ramon is making coffee and singing a Diana Ross song. Gregory comes into the kitchen.)*

RAMON. Good morning, Gregory. The coffee's brewing. I woke up in my diva mode and there is no greater diva than Diana Ross. *(Sings a Diana Ross song.)* I figured you were working out there. I saw the lights. I didn't want to disturb you. How's it going. Don't ask, hunh? *(He sings a Diana Ross song and undulates. He's terrific.)* These are the exact movements that won me my high school talent contest. My big competition was a girl in glasses — Julia Cordoba — who played "Carnival in Venice" on the trumpet. Next to "You Can't Hurry Love" she didn't have a chance. But just in case anybody thought I was too good at Diana, I went into my tribute to Elvis, the title song from *Jailhouse Rock. (He sings from the title song from* Jailhouse Rock* *and dances. He's electric. He remembers the choreography from the movie perfectly.)* I was turning the whole school on. Girls, boys, faculty. I loved it. If I ever get famous like you, Greg, and they ask me when I decided I wanted to be a dancer — no, a great dancer, like you were — I am going to answer, "I remember the exact moment when. It was on the stage of the Immaculate Conception Catholic High School in Ponce in the Commonwealth of Puerto Rico when —" *(He slows down but keeps dancing.)* What's the matter? What are you looking at? You're making me feel weird. Come on, don't. You know me, I'm goofing. "Great dancer you *are.*" I didn't mean it, okay? *(He dances slower and slower, but he has too much machismo to completely stop.)* Fuck you then. I'm sorry your work isn't going well. Bobby told me. But don't take it out on me. I'm just having fun. Sometimes I wonder why we bother, you know? Great art! I mean, who needs it? Who fucking needs it? We got Diana. We got Elvis. *(He has practically danced himself into Gregory and is about to dance away from him at his original full, exuberant tempo when Gregory grabs his wrist.)* Hey! *(Gregory leads him to the sink.)* What are you doing? Let go. *(Gregory throws a switch. We hear the low rumble of the disposal.)* What are you doing? I said. I don't like this. *(Gregory turns off the disposal. He grabs Ramon's other arm and twists it behind his back. At the same time he lets go of his wrist.)* Ow!

GREGORY.   Put your. Um. Hand down the drain.

RAMON.   Fuck you, no!

GREGORY.   Do it.

RAMON.   No, I said. Ow! Ow!

GREGORY.   I said, do it!

* See Special Note on Songs and Recordings on copyright page.

RAMON.   What for?

GREGORY.   You know what for.

RAMON.   I don't.

GREGORY.   You know.

RAMON.   Because of Bobby.

GREGORY.   Because of Bobby? Did you say "Because of Bobby"? What, because of Bobby?

RAMON.   Nothing. Nothing because of Bobby.

GREGORY.   *(Slowly and deliberately.)* Put your hand down the drain.

RAMON.   No. Ow!

GREGORY.   Do it or I'll break it fucking off.

RAMON.   You're crazy. You're fucking crazy. *(Perry enters the kitchen area. Buzz is right behind him.)*

PERRY.   Jesus, Gregory. What are you —?

RAMON.   He wants me to put my fucking hand down the drain.

GREGORY.   Tell them why.

RAMON.   I don't know.

GREGORY.   Tell them why.

RAMON.   He thinks me and Bobby …

GREGORY.   That's why.

PERRY.   Somebody's gonna get hurt fooling around like this.

BUZZ.   Let him go, Greg.

RAMON.   Ow!

GREGORY.   I'll break it.

RAMON.   All right, all right. I'll do it, I'll do it. *(Ramon puts his hand down the drain.)* Go ahead, turn it on, cut my fucking fingers off. *(Gregory lets go of Ramon's arm.)*

GREGORY.   Is that coffee. Um. Ready yet?

BUZZ.   That wasn't funny, Greg.

PERRY.   Are you all right?

RAMON.   That wasn't about me and Bobby. That was about me and you.

GREGORY.   Coffee, Perry?

PERRY.   Thank you.

RAMON.   You're old and you're scared and you don't know what to do about it.

GREGORY. Buzz?

BUZZ. Sure.

RAMON. I'm young and I'm not scared and I'm coming after you.

GREGORY. Ramon?

RAMON. That's what it was about. Yes, please, with milk.

GREGORY. One *café con leche* for Ramon.

RAMON. Thank you.

PERRY. Anyway. My stomach is up in my throat.

RAMON. I knew he wouldn't do it. I knew you wouldn't do it.

BUZZ. Macho man herself here.

RAMON. He's just lucky I didn't pop him one. *(Gregory turns on the disposal. Everyone jumps a little.)*

GREGORY. Sorry. Coffee grounds.

BUZZ. You're not supposed to put them down there.

GREGORY. Live dangerously. That's my. Um. Motto.

PERRY. Anyway. The incident was never mentioned again. Funny, the things we sit on, stuff down. The simplest exchanges take on an entirely different meaning.

GREGORY. Ramon. Would you. Um. Take this up to. Um. Bobby. Thank you.

PERRY. No, not funny. Amazing. *(Gregory returns to the studio, puts the music on, and goes back to work.)* Anyway. We spent all day in bed. We napped, we cuddled. Arthur read the life of Donald Trump. Don't ask. We listened to the rain.

ARTHUR. It's stopped.

PERRY. Of course it's stopped. The day is shot. We'll all go out and get a good moonburn tonight.

ARTHUR. It's not shot. Come on, we're going canoeing.

PERRY. It's dusk. It's practically dark, Artie. No. Absolutely not. We went canoeing. *(They begin to paddle.)*

ARTHUR. I don't believe the rain this summer. First Memorial Day, then the Fourth.

PERRY. It's simple. God doesn't want you to beat me in tennis anymore.

ARTHUR. That's not what it means. It means He doesn't want us to develop skin cancer from overzealous exposure to

His sun in our overzealous pursuit of looking drop-dead good to one another. Look out for that log.

PERRY.   That's big of Him. I see it.

ARTHUR.   After AIDS, he figures we deserve a break.

PERRY.   That's five dollars!

ARTHUR.   I think we've stopped playing that game.

PERRY.   Who won?

ARTHUR.   Not Buzz and James.

PERRY.   How did we manage?

ARTHUR.   Depends on who you slept with.

PERRY.   Fourteen years. I haven't been perfect. Just lucky.

ARTHUR.   I've been perfect.

PERRY.   Sure you have!

ARTHUR.   Do you ever feel guilty?

PERRY.   No, grateful. Why, do you?

ARTHUR.   It used to be nearly all the time. No, first I was just scared. Then the guilt. Massive at first. Why not me? That lingers, more than the fear. We've never really talked about this. Paddle.

PERRY.   I'm paddling.

ARTHUR.   Every time I look at Buzz, even when he's driving me crazy, or now James, I have to think, I have to say to myself. "Sooner or later, that man, that human being, is not going to be standing there washing the dishes or tying his shoelace."

PERRY.   None of us is. Are. Is. Are?

ARTHUR.   I don't know. Are. You're right. It's no comfort, but you're right.

PERRY.   Will be. None of us will be.

ARTHUR.   Paddle, I said.

PERRY.   Why not, not you?

ARTHUR.   That's a good question. I wish I could answer it. *(James and Buzz come into view in a canoe. Buzz is doing the paddling. James is up front.)*

PERRY.   Can we drift a while? Look, there's Buzz and James. Hello!

ARTHUR.   Can we finish something for a change?

JAMES.   I feel guilty. You're doing all the paddling.

BUZZ. Good, I want you to. Look at the turtle!

JAMES. I'm going to miss all this.

BUZZ. Sshh. Don't say that. Sshh. Don't even think it.

JAMES. There's Perry and Arthur.

BUZZ. I don't want to talk to anyone. Just us.

ARTHUR. I think we're back to zero with this thing, but I'm willing to bend my shoulder and start all over again. What else am I going to do with my time? But the fellow next to me with his shoulder to the same wheel isn't so lucky. He gets sick, I don't. Why is that? I think we should both go together. Is that gay solidarity or a death wish?

PERRY. Don't talk like that.

ARTHUR. I will always feel guilty in some private part of me that I don't let anyone see but you, and not even you all of it; I will always feel like a bystander at the genocide of who we are.

PERRY. You're not a bystander.

ARTHUR. If you didn't save the human race you're a bystander.

PERRY. That's crazy. You sound like Buzz.

ARTHUR. That's how I feel.

PERRY. You're not a bystander.

JAMES. Buzz, could we go back now?

BUZZ. Sure, honey.

JAMES. Right away. I'm not feeling terribly well.

BUZZ. You're there.

ARTHUR. Hello! They see us.

BUZZ. We'll see you at dinner!

PERRY. *(To Buzz and James.)* You want to race?

ARTHUR. Perry!

BUZZ. What?

ARTHUR. Jesus.

PERRY. I'm sorry. I wasn't thinking.

BUZZ. *(To Perry.)* What did you say?

PERRY. Nothing! It's all right!

ARTHUR. Let's go in. *(They paddle.)*

PERRY. You're not a bystander.

BUZZ. Grace. I thought he said something about grace.

JAMES.   I think I soiled myself.

BUZZ.   We're almost there. *(He paddles.)*

PERRY.   Anyway. Anyway. That evening. I'm sorry. *(He can't continue.)*

JAMES.   That evening it rained harder than ever. I'll do it. (I hate making someone cry.) There was talk of tar-and-feathering the weatherman.

PERRY.   I'm sorry.

JAMES.   A slight case of the runs, Perry. I'm fine now. My bum is as clean as a baby's. The best is yet to come. The real horror.

BUZZ.   We don't know that.

JAMES.   Yes, we do.

PERRY.   I don't know what came over me.

ARTHUR.   It's all right, come on, Perry. *(They go.)*

JAMES.   I thought I put it very politely. I mean, I could have said, "I shit myself."

BUZZ.   We're all walking on eggshells. I'll draw your bath, luv.

JAMES.   Was that "luv" or "love," luv?

BUZZ.   For people who insist on spelling "valor" with a *u* and using words like "lorry" and "lift," you're lucky we have a lenient immigration. *(He goes.)*

JAMES.   Anyway. (If I'm going to fill in for Perry here, I might as well try to sound like him. Bloody unlikely!) After my bath, Buzz (and I never remotely thought in my wildest imaginings that I would be making love to someone called Buzz and saying things like "I love you, Buzz," or "How do you take your tea, Buzz?"), this same, wonderful Buzz wrapped me in the biggest, toastiest bath sheet imaginable and tucked me safely into that lovely big chair by the window in the corner of our room. I fell asleep listening to my brother play Rachmaninoff downstairs. I would wake up to one of the most unsettling, yet strangely satisfying, conversations of my long/short life. And I will scarcely say a word. *(He closes his eyes. The piano music stops. He stands up and looks down at the chair. He is John.)*

JOHN.   There's no point in pretending this isn't happening.

You're dying, aren't you? There are so many things I've never said to you, things we've never spoken about. I don't want to wait until it's too late to say them. I've spent my life waiting for the appropriate moment to tell you the truth. I resent you. I resent everything about you. You had Mum and Dad's unconditional love and now you have the world's. How can I not envy that? I wish I could say it was because you're so much better looking than me. No, the real pain is that it's something so much harder to bear. You got the good soul. I got the bad one. Think about leaving me yours.

They have names for us, behind our back. I bet you didn't know that, did you? James the Good and John the Bad, the Princes of Charm and Ugly. Gregory keeps a journal. We're all in it. I don't come off very well in there, either. So what's your secret? The secret of unconditional love? I'm not going to let you die with it.

My brother smiled wanly and shook his head, suggesting he didn't know, dear spectators. And just then a tear started to fall from the corner of one eye. This tear told me my brother knew something of the pain I felt of never, ever, not once, being loved. Another tear. The other eye this time. And then I felt his hand on mine. Not only did I feel as if I were looking at myself, eyes half-open, deep in a winged-back chair, a blanket almost to my chin, in the twilight of a summer that had never come, and talking to myself, who else could this mirror image be but me?, both cheeks wet with tears now, but now I was touching myself. That hand taking mine was my own. I could trace the same sinews, follow the same veins. But no! It brought it to other lips and began to kiss it, his kisses mingling with his tears. He was forgiving me. My brother was forgiving me. But wait! — and I tried to pull my hand away. I hated you. He holds tighter. I. More kisses. I. New tears. I wished you were dead. He presses his head against my hand now and cries and cries and cries as I try to tell him every wrong I have done him, but he just shakes his head and bathes my hand with his tears and lips. There have never been so many kisses, not in all the world, as when I told my brother all the wrongs I had done him and he forgave me.

Nor so many tears. Finally we stopped. We looked at each other in the silence. We could look at each other at last. We weren't the same person. I just wanted to be the one they loved, I told him. *(John sits in the chair.)*

JAMES.   And now you will be. *(Lights up on Gregory dancing in the studio. Perry returns to the stage.)*

PERRY.   Gregory was working! The lights in his studio had been burning all that night and now well into the next day. Bobby shuttled food and refreshment from the main house while keeping the rest of us at bay. None of us had ever seen Gregory at work. He'd always kept the studio curtains closed. But this time it was as if he wanted us to watch.

ARTHUR.   We shouldn't be doing this.

RAMON.   Hey, c'mon, quit crowding me.

ARTHUR.   I'm sorry.

RAMON.   Watch Gregory. He is so good. He is so fucking good. I'd give my left nut to work with him.

PERRY.   Ouch.

ARTHUR.   Did you ever tell him that?

RAMON.   I'm in a company.

ARTHUR.   Not his. And I think the expression is "right arm," Ramon. He told Perry he thinks you're a magnificent dancer.

RAMON.   He never told me.

ARTHUR.   What are you two having? A withholding contest? Duck! He'll see us.

RAMON.   I think he knows we're out here.

BOBBY.   Someone's out there, Gregory.

ARTHUR.   He's going to kill you. *(He goes. Gregory finishes the dance. He is exhausted.)*

PERRY.   When Gregory finished, he knew he had made something good, something he was proud of.

GREGORY.   It's done, Bobby. It's finished.

BOBBY.   The whole thing? Beginning, middle, and end?

GREGORY.   Yes! It's even got an epilogue. Give me a hug, for Christ's sake! No, give me a chair. You got an old boy-friend, honey.

PERRY.   He also knew he would never be able to dance it.

Not the way he wanted it to be danced.

BOBBY.   What's the matter?

GREGORY.   I can't do this anymore.

BOBBY.   Your legs just cramped. Here, let me. *(He massages Gregory's legs.)*

PERRY.   It wasn't just his legs. It was everything. Gregory had begun to hurt too much nearly all the time now. He knew he'd never make it through a whole performance.

GREGORY.   Ramon!

BOBBY.   You let him watch?

GREGORY.   I wanted him to watch. Ramon! *(Ramon comes into the studio.)*

RAMON.   I'm sorry, Gregory, I couldn't help myself. But Jesus, where does stuff like that come from? I would give my life to dance something like that solo one day.

PERRY.   Ramon had obviously reconsidered his priorities.

BOBBY.   What are you doing, Gregory?

PERRY.   Gregory was suddenly a forty-three-year-old man whose body had begun to quit in places he'd never dreamed of, looking at a twenty-two-year-old dancer who had his whole career ahead of him.

GREGORY.   You're good, Ramon. You're very good. You're better than I was at your age, but that's not good enough, you should be better.

RAMON.   Don't you think I know that?

PERRY.   What Gregory next said surprised everyone, but no one more than himself.

RAMON.   You mean your solo? In rehearsal? So you can see how it looks?

GREGORY.   It would be your solo at the premiere. New York. Early December.

RAMON.   I don't know what to say.

PERRY.   I can't believe people really say things like that. I mean, all your life you wait for the Great Opportunity and you suddenly don't know what to say. It reminds me of the time I —

RAMON.   Where are you going to be?

GREGORY.   Out front. Watching you.

RAMON. What about...? *(He motions toward Bobby.)*
PERRY. Someone had to bring it up. It wasn't going to be any of us.
BOBBY. What about what?
GREGORY. Ask him.
BOBBY. What's happening? Don't do this to me.
RAMON. I'm asking you.
GREGORY. I'm fine, Ramon. Are you?
BOBBY. What's happening?
RAMON. When do we start?
GREGORY. The fifteenth. Ten A.M.
RAMON. I'll be there on the first.
GREGORY. You won't be paid.
RAMON. Is this a secret? I mean, can I tell people? I want to call my mother. Is that okay? She'll shit. She won't know what I'm talking about, but she'll shit. *(His enthusiasm is spontaneous and infectious. He runs off yelling.)* Eeeeeowww! *¡Dios mio!*
GREGORY. We always said I would stop when it's time.
BOBBY. Time. I hate that word, "time."
GREGORY. It's time, Bobby.
PERRY. You should have seen this man ten years ago, even five. No one could touch him. He's always been some sort of a god to me.
GREGORY. I just want to stay like this, my eyes closed, and feel you next to me, our hands touching. Two blind mice now. I didn't know I was going to do this, honey.
PERRY. Ever since I'd known Gregory, he'd been a dancer. I didn't think I would mind this moment so much.
BOBBY. You did the right thing. *(They stay as Gregory has described them. John appears and stands very close to them.)*
JOHN. This is what Gregory wrote in his journal that day. "Bobby and I made love. We kissed so hard we each had hickeys afterwards. I don't think I'll tell him. When I feel his young body against my own, I feel lucky and happy and safe. I am loved."
GREGORY. Okay.
BOBBY. You ready? *(Bobby and Gregory get up and slowly leave the stage. John stops reading, closes the book, and looks in the direc-*

91

tion Bobby and Gregory have gone.)

JOHN.   "And I am all alone." That's from a song. What song? Anyway. *(He sits and stares straight ahead.)*

PERRY.   Anyway. *(Buzz has returned.)* How's James?

BUZZ.   Don't ask. Like ice. I'm running his tub.

PERRY.   Poor guy. How are you?

BUZZ.   Weary and wonderful. *(Gregory appears.)*

GREGORY.   Who's using all the hot water?

BUZZ.   We are, Gregory, I'm sorry.

GREGORY.   That's all right, that's all right. I'll shower later. Really, Buzz, it's fine. *(He goes.)*

BUZZ.   If this were a musical, that would be a great cue for "Steam Heat." "Really, Buzz, it's fine." "I've got ding! ding! steam heat!" Of course, if this were a musical, there would be plenty of hot water, and it would have a happy ending. Life and Gregory's plumbing should be more like a musical: Today's Deep Thought from Buzz Hauser.

PERRY.   Musicals don't always have happy endings, either.

BUZZ.   Yes, they do. That's why I like them, even the sad ones. The orchestra plays, the characters die, the audience cries, the curtain falls, the actors get up off the floor, the audience puts on their coats, and everybody goes home feeling better. That's a happy ending, Perry. Once, just once, I want to see a *West Side Story* where Tony really gets it, where they all die, the Sharks and the Jets, and Maria while we're at it, and Officer Krupke, what's he doing sneaking out of the theater? — get back here and die with everybody else, you son of a bitch! Or a *King and I* where Yul Brynner doesn't get up from that little Siamese bed for a curtain call. I want to see a *Sound of Music* where the entire von Trapp family dies in an authentic Alpine avalanche. A *Kiss Me Kate* where's she got a big cold sore on her mouth. A *Funny Thing Happened on the Way to the Forum* where the only thing that happens is nothing and it's not funny and they all go down waiting — waiting for what? Waiting for nothing, waiting for death, like everyone I know and care about is, including me. That's the musical I want to see, Perry, but they don't write musicals like that anymore. In the meantime, gangway, world, get off my runway!

PERRY. You're my oldest friend in the world and next to Arthur, my best.

BUZZ. It's not enough sometimes, Perry. You're not sick. You two are going to end up on Golden Pond in matching white wicker rockers. "The loons are coming, Arthur. They're shitting on our annuities."

PERRY. That's not fair. We can't help that.

BUZZ. I can't afford to be fair. Fair's a luxury. Fair is for healthy people with healthy lovers in nice apartments with lots of health insurance, which, of course, they don't need, but God forbid someone like me or James should have it.

PERRY. Are you through?

BUZZ. I'm scared I won't be there for James when he needs me and angry he won't be there for me when I need him.

PERRY. *(Comforting him.)* I know, I know.

BUZZ. I said I wasn't going to do this again. I wasn't going to lose anyone else. I was going to stay healthy, work hard for the clinic, and finish cataloging my original cast albums. They're worth something to someone, some nut like me somewhere. That was all I thought I could handle. And now this.

PERRY. I know, I know. But it's wonderful what's happened. You know it's wonderful.

BUZZ. Who's gonna be there for me when it's my turn?

PERRY. We all will. Every one of us.

BUZZ. I wish I could believe that.

JAMES. *(Off.)* Buzz, the tub!

BUZZ. Can you promise me you'll be holding my hand when I let go? That the last face I see will be yours?

PERRY. Yes.

BUZZ. I believe you.

PERRY. Mine and Arthur's.

BUZZ. Arthur's is negotiable. I can't tell you how this matters to me. I'm a very petty person.

PERRY. No, you're not.

BUZZ. I've always had better luck with roommates than lovers.

PERRY. I think this time you got lucky with both.

JAMES. *(Off.)* Buzz, it's running over.

BUZZ. I adore him. What am I going to do? *(The other men are assembling in the living room.)*

GREGORY. All right, everyone. This is your five-minute call. This is a dress. *(Buzz, Bobby, Arthur, Ramon, and Gregory will get ready to rehearse the* Swan Lake Pas des Cygnes. *This time they will put on tutus and toe shoes. They will help each other dress. Think of a happy, giggly group of coeds. Perry watches from the side.)* John? Are you ready in there?

JOHN. *(Off.)* All set. *(He starts playing.)*

GREGORY. Not yet! Not yet!

RAMON. Okay, let's do it!

GREGORY. Lord, but you. Um. Have big feet, Bobby.

BUZZ. You're heartless. Picking on the handicapped.

BOBBY. I'm not handicapped. Not anymore. I'm visually challenged.

BUZZ. I'm sorry, doll.

BOBBY. That's all right, doll. It took me forever.

GREGORY. John, are you still ready?

JOHN. *(Off.)* Yes, Gregory.

GREGORY. Tuck it in, Arthur.

ARTHUR. I beg your pardon.

PERRY. You see? That's what I keep telling him.

ARTHUR. If you're just going to sit on the sidelines and be a kibitz.

RAMON. Kibitz? What's a kibitz?

BUZZ. It's a place where very old gay Jewish couples go. *(Gregory claps his hands with a choreographer's authority.)*

GREGORY. All right, gentlemen. Line up. From the top.

BUZZ. We're in big trouble.

GREGORY. John? Are you ready?

JOHN. *(Off.)* Yes, for the eighty-fifth time! *(Gregory claps his hands again.)*

GREGORY. Okay, everybody. This is a take. All set, John. *(John begins to play off-stage and they begin to dance. They have improved considerably since they started rehearsing.)* Very good. Very good.

RAMON. Ow! Buzz kicked me.

BUZZ. Tattletale. Shut up and dance.

ARTHUR. That's from *Gypsy*.

BUZZ. That's amazing from an accountant.

BOBBY. How are we looking?

PERRY. Actually, you look like you're having fun.

BOBBY. Well, come on then! *(James enters. He has put on his tutu.)*

JAMES. You started without me.

BUZZ. We thought you were resting.

JAMES. Don't stop. Let me in. *(He links arms with Bobby and joins in the dance. The others are apprehensive about his participation but try not to show it.)* Left! I always want to go right on that step.

BUZZ. If you do and I hear about it...! That was the punchline to a politically incorrect joke nobody dares tell anymore.

ARTHUR. But you will.

BUZZ. Absolutely. Hervé Villechaize, the deceased midget, was talking to Faye Dunaway.

ALL. She's gay, you know.

BUZZ. Keep trying, guys. One of these days you'll get it. Anyway. Hervé and Faye.

PERRY. Anyway. While my friends rehearsed and laughed and I watched and felt envious of their freedom (I couldn't believe that was my Arthur with them! My button-down, plodding Arthur!), something else was happening, too. Something awful. James collapsed. *(Everyone stops as James falters. John keeps playing the piano, off.)*

JAMES. I'm fine. I said, I'm fine! Everybody, please. Back off. I just want to lie down a little.

BUZZ. I'll —

JAMES. No. I'm fine. Don't stop. Go on. You need all the rehearsal you can get. *(He goes.)*

GREGORY. John, will you stop. John, goddamnit! *(The music continues.)*

RAMON. I'll tell him. *(He goes.)*

ARTHUR.   Buzz, maybe you should go with him.

BUZZ.   Maybe you should mind your own business.

ARTHUR.   I'm sorry. *(Ramon returns.)*

RAMON.   John's gone up to him.

BUZZ.   Put on the record. That's how we're going to perform it anyway. The piano is for stop-and-start. We're beyond stop-and-start.

ARTHUR.   We're one short again.

BUZZ.   We'll live. *(He starts taking charge, his way of being in denial about James's condition.)* Let's go. Places, ladies. From the top.

RAMON.   You're being replaced, Gregory.

BUZZ.   Did anyone object to me calling them ladies? Speak now or forever hold your peace.

PERRY.   I object.

BUZZ.   You're not in this piece. *(He claps his hands. This time we hear the Tchaikovsky in the full orchestral arrangement. They being the dance again. The dance continues.)*

PERRY.   I wanted to join them. I couldn't. I just couldn't. I was a dancer once. I was a good dancer. What happened?

GREGORY.   Come on. Um. Perry. We need. Um. You. It's a. Um. *Pas de six.*

BUZZ.   That sounds dirty. I wish it were. *(As the dance proceeds, one by one the men will stop dancing, step forward, and speak to us.)*

PERRY.   I have twenty-seven years, eight months, six days, three hours, thirty-one minutes, and eleven seconds left. I will be watching *Gone With the Wind* of all things again on television. Arthur will be in the other room fixing me hot cocoa and arguing with his brother on the phone. He won't even hear me go.

ARTHUR.   You insisted on keeping the TV on so loud. Wouldn't buy a hearing supplement.

PERRY.   I hate that word, "supplement." They're aids. Hearing aids. They're for old men.

ARTHUR.   Three years later, it's my turn. On the bus. The M-9. Quietly. Very quietly. Just like my life. Without him, I won't much mind.

GREGORY. You're getting behind, Arthur, catch up!

BUZZ. I don't want to think about it. Soon. Sooner than I thought, even. Let's just say I died happy. They'd reissued *Happy Hunting* on CD and I'd met Gwen Verdon at a benefit. She was very nice and I don't think it was because she knew I was sick. Perry and Arthur said, "You know what Ethel Merman is going to do to you, telling everyone she was a big dyke?"

GREGORY. On the beat, Buzz, on the beat. *(James appears.)*

JAMES. I wasn't brave. I took pills. I went back home to Battersea and took pills. I'm sorry, Buzz. *(He goes.)*

RAMON. I don't die. I'm fucking immortal. I live forever. Until I take a small plane to Pittsfield, Massachusetts. I was late for a concert. Nobody else from my company was on it. Just me and a pilot I didn't bother to look at twice.

BOBBY. I don't know.

GREGORY. You —

BOBBY. I don't want to —

GREGORY. You won't be with me.

BOBBY. I'm sorry.

GREGORY. What was his name?

BOBBY. Luke.

GREGORY. That's right, Luke.

BOBBY. You knew that. He knew that. He does that just to…. What about you?

GREGORY. There was no one else. Not even close. You were the last.

BOBBY. I'm sorry, Gregory.

GREGORY. It was my age.

BOBBY. No.

GREGORY. It was my age.

BOBBY. Yes.

GREGORY. You —

BOBBY. I said I don't want to know.

GREGORY. Don't be afraid.

BOBBY. I'm not.

GREGORY.   It will seem like forever.

BOBBY.   I'm sorry I couldn't stay with you.

GREGORY.   I. Um. Bury every one of you. Um. It got. Um. Awfully lonely out here. *(John appears.)*

JOHN.   I didn't change. And I tried. At least I think I tried. I couldn't. I just couldn't. No one mourned me. Not one tear was shed. *(Long pause. No one moves. Finally:)*

PERRY.   Anyway. *(The dance resumes and the Tchaikovsky is heard again. By this final reprise of the dance their precision and coordination is as good as it's going to get.)* It was just about now when the lights went out. *(The music stops and the lights go off abruptly.)* Violet thunderstorms are taken for granted in this neck of the woods. So are power failures when you live as remotely as Gregory. *(Already matches are being struck and candles lit.)* The benefit rehearsal would have to wait.

BUZZ.   There will be no performance of *Ze Red Shoes* tonight. *(More and more candles are being lit.)* When do you expect the power back?

BOBBY.   Are the lights still out? Aaaww! It could be forever.

BUZZ.   You don't have to sound so cheerful. *(The stage is ablaze with lit candles by now.)*

ARTHUR.   You know what's going to happen, don't you? We'll all be sound asleep and the lights will come back on and the music will start playing and we'll all be scared to death. Why is it that when the lights go off the telephones usually still work? Hunh?

BUZZ.   Gay people aren't expected to answer questions like that.

PERRY.   Speak for yourself.

BUZZ.   I was. I usually do. Whose turn is it to do the dishes?

BOBBY.   I'll start.

PERRY.   You cooked.

ARTHUR.   Hey, no fair.

BOBBY.   Who said life was fair? It certainly wasn't a blind person. *(John enters.)*

BUZZ.   How is he?

JOHN.   He's sleeping but he's better. He's a little better.

You've all been so.... There aren't words enough. Can I give anyone a hand? I want you to like me. *(John exits.)*
ARTHUR.   Look out there. It's clearing up. There's a full moon.
PERRY.   This is why people have places in the country.
BUZZ.   Even gay people, Perry.
ARTHUR.   Drop it, you two.
RAMON.   You could practically read by that moonlight. The dishes can wait. Come on, Bobby.
BOBBY.   It's wasted on me. Go on down to the lake. All of you. Make them, Greg. I'll join you.
BUZZ.   He's a saint. He's gorgeous and he's a saint.
GREGORY.   John? We're all going down to the lake.
PERRY.   What's the weather supposed to be tomorrow?
ARTHUR.   More rain. *(Perry, Ramon, Arthur, Buzz, and Gregory move to the rear of the stage, where they sit with their backs to us looking at the moonlight on the lake. Arthur begins to sing "Shine On, Harvest Moon." The others will join in. Bobby is clearing up. James enters. He is wearing a robe. He watches Bobby.)*
BOBBY.   Who's there? Somebody's there.
JAMES.   It's me. Forgive me for staring. You looked very handsome in the moonlight. Very handsome and very graceful. You took my breath away. I'm going to remember you like that. It's James.
BOBBY.   I know. Are you supposed to be down here?
JAMES.   No. And neither are you. There's a full moon and everyone's down by the lake. I saw them from my window. Come on. I'll go with you. *(He takes Bobby by the arm.)* I have a confession to make. I've never been skinny-dipping in the moonlight with a blind American. You only live once.
BOBBY.   If you're lucky. Some people don't live at all. I thought you were scared of that snapping turtle.
JAMES.   I'm terrified of him. I'm counting on you.
BOBBY.   Let's go then.
JAMES.   I have another confession to make. I'm English. I've never been skinny-dipping in the moonlight with anyone.
BOBBY.   I knew that. *(They leave. The front of the stage and*

main playing area are bare. Everyone is taking off his clothes to go swimming now. One by one we see the men at the rear of the stage undress and go into the lake. As they go into the water and swim out, the sound of their voices will fade away. Silence. Empty stage. John enters. He looks back to the lake. He looks up at the sound of a plane overhead. He looks out to us.)

JOHN.   Anyway. *(He looks straight ahead. He doesn't move. The lights fade. Blackout.)*

PROPERTY LIST

ACT ONE

On Stage
Model house
Journal
Telephone
Ashtray
4 soft duffel bags
    (1 with hair dryer)
2 backpacks
    (1 with compact disks, mail and sheet music)
Zabar's bag
Covered casserole dish
Chair
Cigarettes
Lighter

Off Left
Dinner table set with:
    7 plates, spoons, forks, linen napkins, coffee mugs
    2 wine glasses, half full
    2 candles
    bowl
    sugar bowl and creamer
    plates with partially eaten coffee cake
Blanket
Sweater
2 green towels
Dishtowel
Pillow
Coffee pot, full
3 chairs
Buzz's backpack
Bandage

Off Right
3 chairs
Mixing bowl
Wooden spoon
Salad dressing
2 colorful towels

ACT TWO

Off Left
Remote control (on sofa)
Tea cart with:
    book, *Outing America From A to Z*
    book, *Northanger Abbey*
    bowl of potato chips
    cocktail napkins
    pitcher of iced tea
    4 drinking glasses
    blanket
Chair
Ice pack
Plate of cookies
Walkman player and headset
Tube of sunblock
Calculator in gift box
Towel
4 tennis racquets
Journal

Off Right
Hammock
Pad and pencil
Tape measure
Bracelet
Scissors
Leather suitcase

Cake with candles (to be lit)
Party horn
Vanity Fair magazine, with centerfold

ACT THREE

On Stage
3 mugs
Chair
Water bottle

Off Left
Kitchen table with:
    plunger coffee pot, with coffee
    2 mugs
    dishtowel
    sugar bowl and creamer
Chair
5 candles
Umbrella
Coffee mug
Journal

Off Right
Wing-back chair
6 candles
2 pillows
Hand towel

SOUND EFFECTS

Milk bottle breaking
Running water
Piece of cloth being torn
A man relieving himself
Thunder
Car approaching
Door slam
Thunder, distant
Crickets
Car horn, distant
Sounds of a violent altercation (coming from a TV set)
Rumble of a kitchen disposal
Plane, overhead

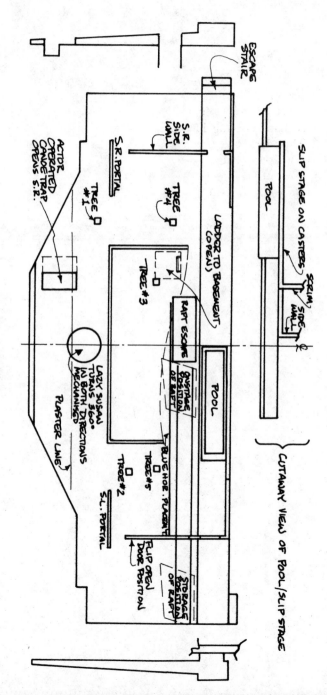

SCENE DESIGN
"LOVE! VALOUR! COMPASSION!"
(DESIGNED BY LOY ARCENAS FOR MANHATTAN THEATRE CLUB)

NEW
PLAYS

THE AFRICAN COMPANY PRESENTS
RICHARD III
by Carlyle Brown

EDWARD ALBEE'S
FRAGMENTS and THE MARRIAGE PLAY

IMAGINARY LIFE
by Peter Parnell

MIXED EMOTIONS
by Richard Baer

THE SWAN
by Elizabeth Egloff

Write for information as to
availability
DRAMATISTS PLAY SERVICE, Inc.
440 Park Avenue South   New York, N.Y. 10016

NEW
PLAYS

THE LIGHTS
by Howard Korder

THE TRIUMPH OF LOVE
by James Magruder

LATER LIFE
by A.R. Gurney

THE LOMAN FAMILY PICNIC
by Donald Margulies

A PERFECT GANESH
by Terrence McNally

SPAIN
by Romulus Linney

*Write for information as to
availability*
DRAMATISTS PLAY SERVICE, Inc.
440 Park Avenue South   New York, N.Y. 10016

NEW
PLAYS

LONELY PLANET
by Steven Dietz

THE AMERICA PLAY
by Suzan-Lori Parks

THE FOURTH WALL
by A.R. Gurney

JULIE JOHNSON
by Wendy Hammond

FOUR DOGS AND A BONE
by John Patrick Shanley

DESDEMONA, A PLAY ABOUT A
HANDKERCHIEF
by Paula Vogel

*Write for information as to
availability*
DRAMATISTS PLAY SERVICE, Inc.
440 Park Avenue South   New York, N.Y. 10016